JOHN EDRICH

# Runs in the Family

As told to DAVID FRITH

Foreword by ALEC V. BEDSER

STANLEY PAUL
*London*

STANLEY PAUL & CO LTD
*178–202 Great Portland Street, London W1*

AN IMPRINT OF THE HUTCHINSON GROUP

London Melbourne Sydney
Auckland Bombay Toronto
Johannesburg New York

★

*First published 1969*



*This book has been set in Baskerville,
printed in Great Britain on Antique Wove paper
by Balding + Mansell Ltd of London and Wisbech,
and bound by Wm. Brendon, of Tiptree, Essex.*

*09 097840 4*

DEDICATED TO

MY WIFE,

JUDITH

# Contents

# Illustrations

# Foreword by Alec V. Bedser

John Edrich is part of that renowned family and how well he has added to the lustre.

He had his great chance in 1959 at Nottingham. He opened the innings and scored 100 and from then he has never looked back.

Test honours came his way and although he had his early set-backs, he has now established himself in the international side. This has been due to his great determination and will to do well. John is not a theorist or one to make excuses. He has always played each innings as it comes. When he had the terrible blow on the head by a ball from Peter Pollock the South African, many thought his international career was over. They did not know John Edrich. He came back and proved to all that his rightful place was in the England side.

I have always known that a one hundred per cent effort would come from John and I wish his book, and himself, every success. It seems a long time since I first saw the shy Norfolk lad arrive at The Oval and I am proud to have known him. He has not changed—except in his ability as a cricketer.

# Introduction

Some of my best friends have put me into hospital. Fred Trueman did it the first time we met. He broke my hand.

Frank Tyson, a scholarly chap, broke it again and a surgeon had to scrounge a piece of bone from my leg to mend it.

A spring-heeled South African called Pollock crumpled me like a puppet without a string, with a broken head.

Big boisterous Charlie Griffith rushed me into a casualty ward with an arm like a balloon.

In India I lay delirious, convinced that I would never again see the Kennington gasometer.

Tear gas made me cry in the gay Caribbean and I just could not understand how the gentle game I learned to play against the Norfolk farmhouse wall could ever lead to things like that.

It did, and I thank the whole world for it; the whole crazy, marvellous world of cricket, full of surprises, high spots and low, from Wagga Wagga to Worcester, Bangalore to Bridgetown, Capetown to Cardiff and Chipping Norton to Clapham (West).

I am tattooed with scars but unfortunately pain is something you cannot remember, it doesn't matter how hard you try. But, remembering, I tingle with the excitement of the moments before the pain, before they chased me off to hospital. And afterwards, I always wanted to go back again.

Cricket has never cheated me. It has given me the life I wanted, in the way I always hoped it would be.

With this book I know I am conforming to fashion. It is something which most cricketers who have been lucky enough to be carried along by the game, sustained by extra rewards and boosted by representative honours, want to do.

I wanted to write it for the young player who feels he might never be getting even only a 'half chance'. But of course it is not for him alone.

The boy in the non-cricketing counties—I'm writing now of cricket in the county championship sense—will know what I mean about having 'only a half chance'.

If he is as lucky as I was with the friends I had who wanted to help, he will of course get every chance. In Norfolk, however, where it all began for me, although it is a Minor county, in the cricketing sense, I know I had an extra special start.

It might be just as well, if at the start, I remind anyone who is inclined to say—'it's all right for him, but . . .', that I was four years on the junior staff of Surrey before I established a place in the county side, which was a fair apprenticeship.

Others will doubtless say that I was given my chance because I was fortunate to inherit the name of Edrich. I must admit this could have been helpful in forging introductions. But I have never once courted friendship or help because of the family name.

It was for this reason that I chose Surrey as the County to give me a break instead of Middlesex where my cousin Bill had carved his own memorable place.

And I chose them at a time when Bill could not possibly have any influence on Surrey to take or reject my application for a trial. Bill was 12,000 miles away playing for England in Australia.

If I was going to make the grade in County cricket and eventually to international honours, I wanted to make it on my own ability. I did not want accusations that the Edrich name had opened doors on my behalf.

Above all I did not want to be the subject of the inevitable comparison which takes place when one member of a family follows an illustrious name into the same business.

It would have happened. The comments of 'John is not as good as Bill', 'He's not a patch on his cousin', 'He doesn't play his strokes like Bill' would have been inevitable.

I do not think I could have stood it. I do not play my cricket like Bill and any comparison would have been unfair. In the same way it was unfair to compare Billy Sutcliffe with Herbert, Richard Hutton with Sir Leonard, Ken Graveney with Tom.

The comparison that will come soon should Denis Compton's son follow along the same lines with Middlesex and Derek Shackleton's son get his county chance, will be just as out of place.

I was determined to make it on my own and I believe I have done so without the help of the Edrich family tradition. I have never once turned to Bill for advice in sorting out my cricketing problems. And there have been many.

At times I doubted whether I would ever make the huge step from county cricket played in front of a few hundred spectators to Test matches before a full arena.

Only five years ago I nearly left the game completely. By then I had played Test cricket for England against both the West Indies and Australians but I was back in County cricket.

I had been given my chance and had been rejected. It did not look as if I would be getting another opportunity.

Two or three years earlier a similar thing had happened. I thought about finding another occupation first and playing first-class cricket when I could as an 'amateur' in the old tradition.

Now all these doubts are behind me. Cricket is my game, my life and my living. I can see where I am going and I can see where the game is heading. I believe the future is brighter than it has been for many years.

Now I want to stay in the game as long as my frame and legs will carry me up the wicket for a sharp single.

Until, if possible, I have scored a 100 centuries. Until Surrey have won the County championship again, the Gillette Cup and the new Sunday League.

Most of all I want to stay in the game until I have been a member of an England side to beat Australia in a series. My life, which at one stage looked empty, is now very full.

I

# The Edrich XI

My grandfather, Harry Edrich, of Manor Farm, Blofield, a village near Norwich, spent his days farming, cricketing and raising thirteen children. One of his sons became my father, Fred, and another the father of Geoff (Lancashire), Brian (Kent and Glamorgan), Eric (Lancashire) and Bill (the famous 'W. J.' of Middlesex and England).

With so much tradition to live up to, my own innings opened in Blofield on June 21, 1937 and by the time I toddled out at the age of five to face my father's lobs, my cousin Bill was already established as a Test cricketer and, as a Squadron Leader in the RAF, had been awarded the Distinguished Flying Cross for a daylight bombing mission.

We went through the motions on a concrete wicket on the farm, where Dad's chief produce was corn and sugar beet—with pedigree pigs a later line.

The cricket pitch behind the farmhouse was only fifteen yards long, a proper length for a small boy learning the fundamentals of batting.

My Uncle George also had a net in his garden, so there was no shortage of opportunity in those dark days (in our particular neighbourhood only two bombs fell, and my main wartime memory is of cadging gum from American Airmen!)

Most cricket-conscious fathers feel their sons are born batsmen, and mine was no exception. He was a useful player and he devoted all the time he could spare to coaching and encouraging me. He never attempted to convert my natural left-handed tendency, and always insisted I should get behind the ball, which came through truly on the hard surface.

We children staged a thousand and one mini-Tests on that concrete pitch. We listened to our heroes in the real game, then tried to emulate them in the meadow. My sister Freda often joined in the contests.

As with most boys who ever sighted three upright sticks, I fancied myself as a fast bowler. In time I became Captain of Bracondale School XI, in Norwich, opening the bowling and averaging 106 with the bat, going in at number four.

According to the scrap-book compiled by my mother, Mr Fred Scott (the headmaster) at one annual prize giving, assessed my school cricketing performances as being as promising as those of my well-known cousins. Years earlier Mr Scott had laid a concrete wicket at the school to foster the obvious talents of cousin Bill when he was a lad. Mr Scott used to predict to my mother that I, too, would follow Bill into the England side. I am happy to have proved him right, if only for the great help he gave me.

When it became clear early in my teens that I would not be destroying six or seven batsmen per innings with my fast stuff, I took to keeping wicket when the chance arose.

I was behind the stumps one afternoon when a batsman got a rustic top edge, and the ball went straight up. I waited below, gloved fingers eager, the whole of my brief career passing before me—and dropped the ball! From that moment I lost my appetite for keeping wicket as well. A batsman I would be!

During the winter I played football with Blofield in the East Anglian League. I had my hour of glory in a match against Mundesley, with six goals from the centre-forward position, but from the age of seventeen my opportunities were restricted, first by my obsession with cricket, and later by National Service. I wanted to concentrate on cricket and my batting began to develop. During Easter holidays I attended coaching sessions at Britannia Barracks in Norwich, conducted by C. S. R. Boswell of Norfolk and Essex.

At the age of fifteen I had made over a thousand runs in a season, most of them for South Walsham, whose batting order was loaded with Edriches; and in one over for

Ingham (a pretty little village near Hickling Broads, where Prince Philip goes duck shooting) against Palmer's School, I hit 28 runs: 6-6-4-6-0-6 in an innings of 116 not-out.

I captained Norfolk Junior Colts that year, when Peter Parfitt, later of Middlesex and England, was also in the side. Henry Blofeld, who played for Cambridge in the 1959 University cricket match and now writes on sport, was another contemporary. I played occasionally on Henry's family's cricket ground at Hoveton, where barbed wire kept the cows out (though if anyone forgot to shut the gate on Friday the outfield could be hazardous on Saturday). The comfortable dressing rooms and the setting made for a pleasant day's cricket.

Two years later, in 1954, when most of my cricket was played under Laurie Barrett's captaincy with Norwich Church of England Young Men's Society, the county selectors noted a 'series of steady performances' from Peter Parfitt of Fakenham Grammar School and myself. We were both chosen to play for Norfolk.

My first two games for the county, against Essex at Frinton and Kent at Sittingbourne, were disappointing, but during Lakenham Cricket Week I made 56 runs against Buckinghamshire, which helped salvage some prestige, and another 50 against Suffolk.

By the end of the season I was top of the Norfolk averages, and I was being talked about locally as some sort of prospect.

I wrote to Lancashire, where Bill's brother, Geoff, had put in a good word, but they could not give me a chance. At that time they were recruiting only from within their own boundaries. I looked towards Middlesex, but something inside me said that Lord's was Bill's stamping ground (and how he stamped, particularly in 1947, in harness with Denis Compton!) I thought I would have more chance exploring fresh fields.

Bill was helping to retain the Ashes in Australia with Len Hutton's 1954–5 MCC side at the time, but his father encouraged me to stand on my own feet, as did my own father who, like many good Norfolk folk, was sorry I planned to leave the county. Some people felt I ought to gather experience with Norfolk in Minor County competition before the Army conscripted me for two years' National Service.

Nevertheless, I sounded out the Surrey club. In his reply Brian Castor, the Secretary, made it clear he did not wish to dampen my ardour. He explained, however, that Surrey would have to gain the sanction of Norfolk County Cricket Club, and an authentic recommendation would be required.

Laurie Barrett, the Norfolk Captain, gave Surrey the recommendation they needed, and in 1955, still never having seen a first-class match, I reported to the nets at Kennington Oval. I still recall the date, April 15.

At last! This was what I wanted and now I would find out if I was being driven by an honest belief in myself, or whether I was over-estimating a degree of talent in the hope of sharing some of the fame which the Edrich name had already achieved in cricket.

There was no doubt what actually precipitated me towards The Oval and anyone who has tried to start a farm tractor on a freezing January morning, will understand! Winter is always an awfully long time and for a young lad who preferred firm green turf to ploughed fields and who despised the cold and wanted only the sun on his back, that tractor made up my mind. The next day I took a train to London and, I hoped, towards a life which would keep me in the sunshine. Such is the optimism of youth but even on that January morning, when I discovered it was just as cold on the London pavements as in the Norfolk field, I found nothing depressing about The Oval. I was seeing it for the first time. I had never seen a cricket field so large and, although it was empty and quiet and the gas holders grey and sombre, I was very impressed. I knew then that I had not made a mistake in coming and as I went in to talk things over with Brian Castor I hoped that he, too, would feel the same.

Tony Lock was sitting in the Secretary's office, and I remember this red-headed hero of Surrey and England expressing the hope (surely not serious!) that I wasn't a left-arm spinner wanting his place in the team.

Somehow I found my way back to Liverpool Street station, thence Blofield, but I came eagerly back to The Oval, as arranged, in April.

At the nets, set up on the edge of the ground, I began by bowling a wildish ball full-pitch into the back of the netting, which brought a frown to the face of Andrew Sandham, the Surrey Coach, who stood nearby in his MCC tourist blazer. His was a dear old face I was due to see much of in the years ahead. There were other famous faces that day. Jim Laker, Arthur McIntyre, Peter Loader, Tony Lock, the Bedser twins. To me they had all been mere photographs in the newspapers.

I had never known anything like this intensive, well organised net practice. The second team players bowled to me—Mike Willett, the Pratt brothers, Dennis Cox, Harry Kelleher, Dave Halfyard, fellows who, in a county side not so top-heavy with talent, would have formed a formidable attack.

It was interesting to face Dave Halfyard again in 1968 after he had been through several careers. He left Surrey for Kent in 1956, but suffered a bad leg injury in a car accident some years later. It seemed to be all over for him. Subsequently he joined the panel of first-class umpires, but while wheeling down a few balls at the nets, he demonstrated that he could still be a very useful bowler, and Nottinghamshire signed him up. I admire his guts in fighting his way back.

The fortnight of pre-season activity ended, and the senior Surrey side went away on their County Championship campaign. For the first time I found there was no automatic place for me in a cricket team. From being a regular member of school and village teams in Norfolk, I now felt rather on the outside looking in. In my innocence, I was disappointed that there was no place for me in the County side immediately.

My batting needed to improve a lot, of course. So did my fielding. Fortunately I was about to benefit from some of the wisest counsel in the land.

Most of my new team mates knew Surrey very well and as the season wore on I, too, became familiar with the lovely local grounds in many parts of my adoptive county. Travelling around for Club and Ground games we were a very happy crowd. I found that most players were referred to only by nick-names and I was tagged 'Edie' and have been so ever since.

I was surprised at the number of good cricket grounds all in one county: Streatham, Beddington, Cheam, Richmond, Sutton, Mitcham, Reigate, and many more, all with strong teams containing young men who could not or would not commit themselves to cricket as a living.

On many a lonely night, however, I asked myself if I had done the right thing in moving to London. I felt homesick, and in the almost anonymous setting of the junior side, despite the genuine friendliness, I sometimes felt lost. The family were far away. My successful days at the wicket now went unnoticed to them because there was no local Press coverage. All I could do was write letters and hope that at home they appreciated the situation.

Of course I was far from being the first person born outside the County to play for Surrey. Great players who were born elsewhere include Hayward and Hobbs (Cambridge), Lock-wood (Notts), Jardine (India), F. R. Brown (Peru), Laker (Yorks), May, Barrington and the Bedser twins, all born at Reading.

The comparisons to which a young player is exposed are probably more stark in cricket than many other sports be-cause the success or failure of a side depends so much on individual performances. However, because the spotlight is so intensely focussed on individuals it is possible for the youngster to learn, and learn quickly. He is vulnerable to all influences. He is also affected by atmospheres and my first visit to Lord's was certainly part of my conditioning. I was just eighteen and made 68 for Surrey 2nd XI. For some seasons I enjoyed batting there but during the past few sea-sons the bounce of the ball has been often uneven and run-getting much more difficult.

By the end of the 1955 season, with 762 runs in the book, I headed the Surrey 2nd XI averages, and thought 'So far, so good'. The Army had not called me up immediately after my eighteenth birthday, but spared me until December 8, 1955, another important date in my book.

Andrew Sandham had taken over where my father and 'Bossie' Boswell had left off. I had a lot of rough edges. He analysed my every movement, paying special attention to the backlift, which needed raising.

Mr Sandham tried getting me to hold the bat well in the air as the ball was delivered, but I just could not get the hang of that. I might have become more elegant in attack if my backlift had increased, but my preoccupation then was with keeping the ball out at all costs.

I managed some slight modification, but the backlift has never been very high. I depend a lot on the power of my forearms and wrists.

My stance at the wicket has its peculiarities, but it was never forced upon me. The high right shoulder and straight right arm come easy, and I believe the reassuring glance down at my bat as the bowler turns to run in aids my concentration. It has been suggested that I'm making sure the bat is still there, and perhaps this isn't far from the truth!

The Oval is a home to me now, but I still recall the first time I wandered through The Oval Long Room, with its paintings and photographs and ancient scorecards. I began to realise what a history the game of cricket possessed and what a rich tradition The Oval, in particular, could boast.

I met illustrious old players such as Sir Jack Hobbs, Herbert Strudwick and Errol Holmes, all very helpful to an eager novice. This great new world was placing all sorts of wonderful experiences before me. My first grand dinner was at the Grosvenor House Hotel—a splendid occasion to celebrate Surrey's fourth successive Championship, attended by many celebrated people. I was beginning to realise that cricket involved more than bats, balls and stumps.

Surrey at that time were having a great run, winning one Championship after another. The club abounded in personalities and Test cricketers, and more than once I wondered how I could ever begin to find a place among such distinguished company.

They were strange days for a country boy. Accommodation had been the first problem at the start of the season. Frank Ward, a friend of mine whose parents lived in Blofield, arranged to find digs for me at Crofton Park, a crowded suburb of South-east London, so different from the breezy meadows of my native Norfolk.

One evening I waited self-consciously with my two suitcases by the Hobbs Gates for Frank to arrive in his old Vauxhall. We found our way to the little flat, which was above a motor-cycle shop. The landlady announced that there was no room to spare at that time. I was desperate, and we persuaded her to let me have the Put-U-Up in the front room. All that season I had to wait for the other residents to turn in before I could make my bed.

Often too, I travelled in the back of Mike Willett's boat-shaped motor car. Eventually I bought a vehicle of my own, a 1936 Morris tourer, which got me around—sometimes much too swiftly, as when the brakes failed down Reigate Hill on the way to a Surrey Club and Ground game. The master cylinder had run dry, and only frantic pressure on the hand-brake prevented a hideous accident.

I achieved nothing of note for Surrey 2nd XI until late in July, when our opponents at The Oval were Norfolk. I knew I had to succeed. In the first innings I made only 28, but did much better in the second, when we needed 159 against the clock. I hit 21 runs off the last seven balls to see us to victory, finishing 70 not out.

That innings started a good spell for me as my last civilian summer for two years drew to a close. Several sixties, together with participating in a pulsating return win over Norfolk at Lakenham, led to my first hundred for Surrey 2nd XI, against Essex at The Oval, where I was eventually caught by Brian Taylor off Barry Knight, two men of whom the cricket world was to hear much in the years ahead.

All these runs came after I had been promoted to number three in the order, with one opportunity of opening the innings (when Tony Brown, the popular Beddington club player was absent against Kent, and I made 62).

I got to know Tony very well. By then I was living at Tulse Hill, and I spent many an evening at his home in Streatham discussing cricket. He was very helpful and a few years later he was responsible for me putting my name to the bats made by County Sports of St Neots. Laurie Fishlock, of Surrey and England, had done so before me. These fine, hardwood bats are known around the country as 'Brown Bombers', and a number of County and Test cricketers use them.

In the autumn of 1955, before I entered the Army, came one further highlight. I played for the Edrich Family XI against a Norfolk XI at Lakenham, a game staged in aid of Geoff's Testimonial Fund.

This was the third Edrich family cricket match, and my first. In 1938 the proceeds went towards the Blofield Recreation Ground Fund; in 1947 the RAF Benevolent Fund benefited. This time, for his brother Geoff, Bill hit 167 not out, which was exactly 167 runs more than he scored in the corresponding fixtures in 1938—the year he reached a thousand by the end of May.

In 1955, in my initiation into tribal cricket, I made a paltry 14 runs for the clan.

It is probably worth recording that in 1938 I attended the match, though understandably at the age of fifteen months, and, slumped in my father's arms, I gathered no lasting impression! The game went on in spite of drizzle, but the crowd were disappointed when Bill, the man of the hour, was well caught at slip first or second ball.

Thirty years later, I appreciated Bill's feelings when in my own benefit game at Dereham, I was caught sweeping at a wide one after making only a handful of runs. When the bowler appealed I instinctively murmured something that W. G. Grace had first said many decades before: 'These people have come to see me bat today!'

The Umpire was unmoved. Up went the judicial finger. They take their cricket seriously in Norfolk!

2

# First season

My entry into full-time first-class cricket after two years National Service had a fairy-tale touch about it. It is all history now, but the memory of that 1959 season is still vivid. In all the grades of cricket in which I had played until that time I had never done so well as I did in that opening season. Perhaps it was the excellence of the pitches that made it possible. To date I had been batting on many indifferent wickets, but the pitch at Trent Bridge, for example, had me almost gasping at its perfection.

Added to this, the weather was consistently fine that summer, and the games, being stretched over three days, enabled me to plan each innings. There was no need for early rashness.

Knowing less about cricket pitches than I do now (and probably being better off for my ignorance!), I was untroubled by the age-old complex of 'how it would play'. We just didn't talk about it. My full concentration was applied to putting the bat to the ball.

In May, 1959, I was taken with Surrey to Nottingham, and included in the eleven when Dave Fletcher and Tom Clark were unfit. We spotted the cricket ground from the train as we entered Nottingham, and someone recalled that Dave Fletcher had scored 194 there in his second game for Surrey back in 1947, when Stan Squires, Jack Parker and Errol Holmes also made centuries in a total of 706 for four.

Surrey were put in to bat by Reg Simpson and I opened with Micky Stewart on a hazy Whit Saturday morning, with a large crowd eagerly waiting for young John Cotton and Ian

Davison and not-so-young Arthur Jepson to roll us over cheaply.

I kept my head down and watched for scoring chances. We were made to fight for every run, and after an hour we had a modest 39 on the board.

Micky was caught with the total of 46, and Ken Barrington made only 4 but, by now, I was getting my drives and sweeps away and, with Bernie Constable at the other end, I reached 50 with a sweep off Forman, the left-arm spinner.

During the afternoon batting became easier, and in one over I hit Forman to the cover boundary three balls in succession. After Bernie Constable left I shared a stand of almost 100 with Mike Willett and at last, after nearly four hours batting, I reached my century.

I was caught behind for 112 off the last ball before tea, and half an hour from the close Alec Bedser declared at 350 for seven. Mike Willett had gone on to a handsome 72 and, whichever part of the land the spectators came from, I should have thought this a fair day's entertainment. That evening, of course, I was walking on air.

Notts almost caught up with us on first innings. Reg Simpson made 103 and Winfield 98 against an attack worth listing: Loader, the Bedsers, Laker and Lock, plus Barrington. We needed a lot of runs again in the second innings, and now, feeling confident, I found the going much easier, though the scoring rate was not sensational. I put on 221 with Ken Barrington, who had made a century in each innings against Warwickshire the previous week and who, at one stage, looked as if he might reach 1,000 runs in May. Ken remarked between overs, when I had made thirty or forty: 'You can get another hundred here if you try'.

Certainly the circumstances were right once again. My personal tension had eased and I just kept batting. Kenny's judgment was correct. The second hundred came—in slightly better time than the first. Soon afterwards sections of the crowd began to barrack us. The local people wanted a declaration that would let Notts back into the game.

But Alec Bedser, leading the side in Peter May's absence,

knew the wicket was still perfect and Notts were set 273 in 140 minutes. We were given the 'bird' as we walked out to the field, and the game inevitably was drawn.

By then I couldn't care too much about anything. Even if the wicket was hard, even if the bowlers weren't Test match bowlers, with 112 and 124 in only my second game for Surrey, I had done all that I demanded of myself and more.

The telegrams piled up and comparisons, as I suppose was inevitable with so much publicity for cricket, were made with cousin Bill's early achievements. Some newspaper correspondents confused him as being my uncle or my brother and in one case, my father!

But the joy was quickly tempered by the thoughts which raced through my mind: would this be considered a flash in the pan? More important: *was* this a flash in the pan?

We returned to The Oval and I made a few dozen runs against Glamorgan, receiving a chilling warning already that I was being put under the microscope. Some of the opposition and several Press men noticed my slash outside the off-stump and identified it immediately as a glaring weakness.

Somerset visited us, and we were kept in the field all day while Lomax, McCool, Wight and Graham Atkinson all made fair scores. I was not enjoying fielding at this stage. I found it very exacting hour after hour, and I was conscious of the need for improvement. In fact, knowing my limitations as a fielder, I became ridiculously tense.

I disgraced myself that day against Somerset by missing a catch off Tony Lock's bowling at short square-leg before lunch and later in the afternoon I fluffed another chance given by Colin McCool, the ball bouncing from my shoulder over the boundary line for six!

To cap it all, I went out with Micky Stewart that evening to reply to Somerset's 331 and was bowled 'through the gate' for nought. The game was showing me its other face.

Colin McCool, Somerset's leg-spin and googly bowler from Australia, ran through our first innings. To date he was the finest spin bowler I had seen, though it was not until the second innings that I faced him.

We needed 223 to win on a pitch that was taking quite an amount of spin. This time luck was with me.

Micky Stewart and I made 191 for the first wicket—104 each, mine not out. In my naivety I struck McCool's googly—to a right hander that is—across the line to mid-wicket, but it paid off.

My next innings, against Kent, also at The Oval, resulted in 103 runs after I was missed very early and I shared a long partnership with Peter May, who, because of illness, played very little that year. It was an education to bat with him, especially when he was in full flow. We were all very sorry when he retired. He had such enormous natural ability differing from most other great batsmen, however, in that he played his shots right from the start of his innings. Either he came off or he did not and he was such a wonderful judge of strokes that he succeeded more often than he failed.

That century I collected while batting with Peter May was my fourth in seven innings. I reached the 100 by swinging Jack Pettiford to the boundary.

I was just 22. I was full of confidence. For four years I had served my apprenticeship. But for two years on National Service, I might have received my chance earlier.

Certainly no batsman, in his first full season, could hope for better weather conditions than I had in 1959. Indeed, it was the best summer of my career.

The runs continued to come, mainly at The Oval, for which my attachment deepened almost every innings. Against Yorkshire in Bernie Constable's benefit match, I opened my score with a boundary off Fred Trueman, who bowled with all his usual life, and hit me a few times.

This was my first confrontation with Fred, who greeted me as I walked out to bat: 'Morning lad. We haven't seen you before, have we?' Whether this was part of his psychological campaign, I don't know, but his physical hostility was there all right! I had never experienced such bouncers before in my life.

Facing one of the greatest fast bowlers of all time, I didn't know whether to stick or twist, as Kenny Barrington often says. I was struck on the shoulder, and up and down my arms, and in the midriff. I know he was paying special attention to me as a new boy; he bowled at top speed.

After having been singled out and given this torrid 'going-over', I was glad to come away with 76 runs.

Mind you, there was an occasion when Fred bowled me an over of leg-spinners! We were playing Yorkshire at Bramall Lane. The track wasn't helping Freddie and, at the end of an over, I said to him: 'Not much hope for you here, Fred'. 'No, I might as well bowl leg-spinners' he replied. 'You do that!' said I, never dreaming he would. At least I survived that over. If I had got out, I would never have heard the last of it.

Fred was always a bit susceptible to a batsman's 'sympathy'. If I said to him; 'Bad luck, Fred, this wicket's no good for you', I could be certain he would soon be telling me that he hadn't had so many catches dropped in the slips all season or, asking how they expected him to bowl on such slow tracks? I may even have talked him out of bowling flat out to me a few times.

Fred could be furious in every sense of the word. He was once timed to work up a maximum of 84·6 mph through the air and 73·5 mph off the pitch, which doesn't exactly give a batsman much time to change his mind!

Apart from despatching me to Bradford Infirmary the first time we met on his native heath, Fred has thumped me on most parts of the body at one time or another. I am not complaining. It was all part of his job to test me with the full range of his armoury.

Sometimes Freddie niggled me, as he did during a 'purple patch' I had in 1965. I scored something like 1,300 runs in nine innings that summer, and one of those knocks was against Yorkshire at Bradford.

They had left us so many runs to get on a bad wicket that it was more a case of survival than victory for us. But when Fred cracked me on the shoulder with a nasty, kicking ball, the pain goaded me into response.

I struck him straight into the stand over mid on. Fred glowered and roared 'Bloody desperation shot'. He bowled again and this time I hooked him over the mid wicket boundary for another six. An over or so later he hurled down a bouncer and I lashed it over my shoulder into the pavilion.

Fred still maintained it was all desperation on my part. He wouldn't accept that I was riding my luck. That was Fred. He hated all batsmen—and it was this streak of ruthlessness which made him such a great bowler. Off the field, he was always ready for a 'jar' and some earthy humour. He kept his 'hate' strictly for bowling.

I am sorry Fred has gone from the county scene. He was an entertainer and that's the type we need. Still, he'll not be lost altogether. He has arranged to play a lot of one-day cricket.

I was far from satisfied with certain aspects of my technique in that miniature 1959 Test match against Yorkshire. For one thing I knew that I had to formulate a policy for dealing with fast bouncers. Most small men need to hook well and I had always been able to hook quite naturally and safely, but I found I could not do so against such express deliveries as from Fred.

The vital decision had to be whether to hook or duck. This was the split-second answer that had to be found instinctively. There could be no halfway measure.

So we moved on from the electric atmosphere of the Surrey–Yorkshire match to the comparative peacefulness of Guildford, where I took 126 off Cambridge University.

By the first week in July I had scored seven centuries and my first representative selection came in being chosen for the Players against the Gentlemen at Lord's. I suppose this marked the end of my beginning. It certainly marked the end of my glut of runs.

My selection brought a shower of congratulations from many people, among them Andy Sandham, that great cricketer and fine man who had watched me in the nets on my first morning at The Oval. Congratulating me on being selected for the Gents *v* Players he told me, with absolutely no rancour, that in all his long and distinguished career, he had never played in the G *v* P game at Lord's. I realised again, how very fortunate I was to be picked, in my first season of championship cricket.

I opened for the Players with Geoff Pullar, another left hander, and shared 40 for the first wicket. An unusual coincidence was that the Gents' opening pair, Raman Subba Row and Bob Barber, were also left-handers.

Shortly before stumps I was caught at short-leg for 32 by Donald Carr, then Derbyshire's captain, now Assistant Secretary of MCC. The innings was saved next day when Brian Close and Ray Illingworth hit 184 for the seventh wicket.

Their partnership helped put the pressure on the amateurs, but another batsman rose to the occasion: Mike Smith thrashed 166, passing 2,000 for the season and setting his sights on an eventual 3,000. How Mike batted that summer! 3,245 runs—six hundred more than his nearest rival and top of the national averages.

In the end we were set 149 in 80 minutes by Peter May's declaration, and the game petered to a draw.

For me, Old Man Fate was sitting waiting just round the corner. Surrey went to Bradford in July and I had my first glimpse of a Yorkshire crowd. And it wasn't much more than a glimpse either.

I walked out with Tom Clark into the Bullring (as Bradford cricket ground is known) to open the innings on the Saturday morning, and soon the biggest noise I had ever heard on a cricket field erupted as Tom was bowled by Fred Trueman for one. Ken Barrington entered, and the ground was electrified with tension. Here we were, seven-year Champions, pitting our wits and strength against the pride of Yorkshire who, over the decades, had known a thing or two about the art of being County Champions.

I got down the batting end again, and Fiery Fred roared in, black hair flying about, body rocking so powerfully. Whoosh! I bit my lip as the pain spread from a damaged knuckle.

The very next ball also reared horribly and cracked the bottom hand again. The pain intensified. The knuckle began to throb. I faced up again, but soon, slashing at Close, I was taken by Phil Sharpe, a recent Army colleague, at slip.

I was hustled off to Bradford Infirmary, where a suspected

fracture was confirmed. After hanging around there all afternoon I had my hand put into plaster.

The late Sandy Tait, Surrey's popular masseur and general assistant, was sitting among a group of Yorkshiremen in the hotel lounge that evening. He was having to listen to a lot of patriotic Yorkshire cricket talk. Eventually, being a proud Surrey man, he excused himself from the gathering, reappearing minutes later clothed like an ancient Roman—not in a toga, but in Surrey's large County Championship pennant. He sat down with a minimum of fuss, silencing the group who were thunderstruck!

Sandy Tait in his flowing pennant and I scowling in my plaster must have looked a weird pair.

Sandy was a keen practical joker in our dressing room, and often a victim, too. But he usually came off best. He had a chastening habit of sewing up the trouser legs, which may have explained the occasional tardiness of certain Surrey players into the field!

An incident which did leave poor old Sandy second best took place when Alec Bedser and some other players asked for a salt bath one Sunday in Taunton. Sandy trudged round the town looking for salt. Late in the afternoon he puffed his way back to the hotel with half a hundredweight as ordered. Unfortunately the team had given him up for lost and had gone to play golf. As far as I know that sack of salt is still where Sandy dropped it in disbelief.

Because of my hand injury at Bradford—by the way six wickets in each innings by Peter Loader enabled us to win by 48 runs—I missed six games, including the one against the Indians who were hammered so mercilessly and lost all five Tests that year.

The way things had been going for me before my injury I thought I might have been picked for either the fourth or the fifth Test matches. Even now I recall the disappointment I felt at not being included in the long list of 29 'possibles' considered for the MCC tour that winter to the West Indies.

There are many players, never selected for Test cricket, but more accomplished than others who have worn an England Cap. There is room for only so many batsmen and bowlers. How many players, forced into the shadows by the great of their days, would not have been the best in an earlier or later time?

Some players rightly can be acclaimed, among the best of all time; others of us must be, indeed should be, grateful for what we are in our own time.

Others, however, can feel that fate was not exactly on their side. Phil Sharpe, for instance, must be one of the best players ever to turn out for Yorkshire. I just cannot understand why he has not scored those few more runs which would have assured him a regular Test place. One view is that at crucial moments he does not use his feet enough.

His colleague Jackie Hampshire could be one of the great players of the world. If he had played his cricket in the West Indies, Australia or South Africa he would have been a Test star for some years because he is at his supreme best when the ball is coming on to the bat.

Roger Prideaux the Northants skipper must have wondered if he would ever get a cap and Alan Jones of Glamorgan is probably the most neglected opener in the championship. A 2,000-runs-a-year man, he should surely have been given his chance during the years when England were searching for opening batsmen. Jones and Prideaux must have felt they deserved their chance during 1967 when in six Test matches of that year, against India and Pakistan, England tried six different pairs of openers but preferred to reshuffle the side rather than look for new men.

I could list another dozen with similar credentials. No, if there is anything wrong with English cricket it is certainly not a lack of individual talent.

England has often shown a reluctance to place trust in youth, though in other cricketing countries young players get an early chance. Perhaps things are gradually going to change here. I hope so.

So the broken knuckle finally settled things for me. There was only speculation now as to what might have been; the talk had been exciting while it lasted. Now, instead of playing cricket each day as the sun shone and perhaps even gaining an England Cap, I was travelling to the clinic for treatment.

My hopes of going to the West Indies had vanished through the injury but when I came back to the first-class game at Old Trafford, Manchester, I was anxious to find form without delay. But my 5 was lowest score of the first innings, and 29 in the second did nothing to increase my satisfaction, nor that of Surrey, who lost by 10 wickets.

Old Trafford has always been an unprofitable ground for me. I have never made a fifty there, and when in 1968 I was run out for 49 in the first Test against Australia I began to think that the gods who watch over Lancashire cricket had no liking at all for the left-handed Surrey opening batsman!

Soon September came around and Northants played us at The Oval. By drawing the previous game against Middlesex while Yorkshire won at Hove, we lost our chance of an eighth successive championship title. After our seven-year lease of the title this was not very acceptable. Our aim had to be to beat Northants in order to secure second place.

I opened with Brian Parsons on a hard, green coated wicket, with Frank Tyson banging the ball down at such speed that it was thumping into the distant wicket keeper's gloves still on the way up!

Brian, a Brighton college boy, who won Blues at Cambridge, and I formed the smallest opening pair in the country He was five foot seven and I only an inch taller.

After taking a long time over 6 runs, I was struck on the hand by Tyson and the base knuckle of my index finger was broken again. A day or so before Christmas I had an operation. Mr Bill Tucker, who had worked so many wonders for sportsmen (including introducing me to Judy, my future wife, at a party) carried out an arthroplasty of the metacarpophalangeal joint of my left index finger. In other words he removed a tiny piece from my leg and used it to remake the knuckle joint. I awoke to find my leg plastered and my left hand temporarily out of action, thanked Bill profusely, and announced my intention of going home to Norfolk for Christmas.

What an apparition I must have presented when I stopped my car for petrol at a country garage that night! Pale of face, hand bound up, and having to lift my left leg off the clutch pedal. I might have been an escapee from a horror film as I limped on my walking stick to stretch the plaster!

I worked on the farm that winter as well as I could. When the plaster was taken off and I saw my finger once more I instantly gave up hope of playing cricket again. The finger was black! And it was swollen more than Jim Laker's had ever been after even the longest, hardest season's off-spin bowling.

But it settled down and has not bothered me since. The finger is thicker than it was, but I suffer no hindrance from it.

Back in October, Stuart Surridge had taken Surrey to Rhodesia on a goodwill tour, and we played two matches: one at Salisbury and the other at Bulawayo where, despite my knuckle disability preceding the operation I made 151 after Joe Partridge, the Springbok swing-bowler, had been mainly responsible for dismissing us for 75 in the first innings.

While staying at the Victoria Falls Hotel, I shared a ground-floor room with Tony Lock, who seemed to be accident-prone. First his mosquito net collapsed all over him. Then, on one hot night we left the windows open to gather what breeze there happened to be. Unknown to us, a lion was loose and prowling around the grounds. We slept all through the hullabaloo, and you can imagine how we felt the next morning when team-mates pointed out the beast's paw-prints. It had passed immediately beneath our low window! Even if the lion had peered in, I suspect it might have been put off by Tony's peeling bald head!

On another occasion we were exploring Victoria Falls and had to cross some muddy pools. Most of the lads got across without any bother, but 'Lockie' fell in and had to spend the evening in his room reading yet another of his favourite cowboy books while his suit was cleaned.

I have gone into the 1959 season in detail because it was

John Edrich, Surrey and England, in action during the fifth Test match against Australia in August 1968

*Above* Missed! Wicket-keeper Wally Grout takes the ball but fortunately Edrich did not get a touch. England *v* Australia, Lord's, 1964. Edrich went on to make 120

*Left* Edrich run out for 99, Surrey *v* Somerset at the Oval, 1963. Harold Stephenson is the wicketkeeper very important in its way. It was an unusual beginning for me. Often a batsman eases himself into the county side gradually, but, looking back, it seems as if I bashed the door down and marched in still with Norfolk mud clinging to my boots. Yet it didn't all happen quite so suddenly. My turn had been a long time coming.

Peter May awarded me my county cap and Bernie Constable told me 'Well another few years and it'll be your benefit year!'.

Benefits are for middle aged cricketers! It was all too far off and unrealistic yet in 1968 when I rolled up my sleeves for all the industry involved in a benefit season (and winter, around clubs, pubs and dance halls) those ten years seem to have flashed past.

# 3

# Missed chances

At the age of 24 I glimpsed the greatest prize of all—a place in the England team of 1961 against Australia. Ted Dexter had injured a knee and a replacement batsman was wanted.

We were en route from Northampton to Taunton and had stopped at the little Berkshire town of Farringdon for lunch when Micky Stewart found a telephone call waiting for him. He was asked to release me for stand-by duty against Richie Benaud's 1961 team and delightedly I switched direction towards London to collect more kit for a five-day match, at Edgbaston. As events transpired I was not wanted. Ted Dexter was passed fit and proved it by hitting 180.

Perhaps it was all for the best because almost immediately I was ill with tonsillitis and would probably have had a most uncomfortable début.

Another three years passed before I found myself in the squad to oppose Australia. This time it was at Nottingham, and we had a practice session on the afternoon before the Test began. I wish now that we hadn't!

Jim Parks threw a wide ball. I trod on it and twisted my right ankle. Bound to be all right in the morning, I told myself. It just had to be. But it wasn't. I awoke early and got straight up. I could barely walk and, after trying unsuccessfully to get my boot on, I was not too popular when I had to tell the selectors that I was a non-starter. Their concern, quite properly, was that I should have told them immediately any doubt had arisen about being fit. This would have given them a chance to have called up a standby replacement. Looking back I know it was my anxiety not to be disappointed again, against the Aussies, as I had been when I was the standby for Ted Dexter three years before, which kept me silent. It was also unfair on Fred Titmus, who, although he never shirks a challenge and is one of the best all-rounders ever to play for England, was sent in to open the innings in the inevitable last minute reshuffle of the side.

I returned home, dejected and properly chastened. At the time of writing I have still not played in a Test at Trent Bridge.

My hour finally came. I was named for the second Test, at Lord's, and, with the two earlier disappointments at the back of my mind, I immediately began to wonder whether I'd be playing this time, or if yet another twist of fate (or ankle) would intervene. After the first two days had been washed out, I had visions of not getting an innings but, when things did get under way at last on the Saturday we dismissed Australia for 176, Ted Dexter having put them in to bat. Fred Trueman shot half of them out in his own special, outswinging way.

That evening I walked out with Ted Dexter. It was his own decision to try to fill the breach by Boycott's absence due to illness, but Ted, perhaps a little too free to be an opening batsman, was yorked for 2.

I was never more conscious than around this time that I was not cast in the same mould as the Dexters, Mays and Cowdreys. They were and are great natural batsmen with an uncommon quality in their movements and judgment that sets them apart. Only over the last three seasons or so have I felt myself a matured Test cricketer. Previously, and even on that memorable June day at Lord's in 1964, I considered myself as an able county cricketer—no more than that. At the very top—in Test matches—I had to struggle for runs. I had to graft, and in this first Test appearance against Australia there were no easy runs to be had.

I was about 15 not out overnight, with the Sunday, my twenty-seventh birthday, intervening. And on the second morning's play, when Cowdrey and Barrington were both prised out in the first hour, England's position looked insecure.

I had started the day with 3 runs off the edge, but now came a steadying reminder of my early Norfolk days as Peter Parfitt came through the gate. We had played together for Norfolk Junior Colts in the early 'fifties, and now we were batting for England at Lord's.

Family and friends have told me there was a lot of excitement in The Globe, our local pub in Blofield (often referred to as 'The Edrich Arms'!) as Peter and I doubled the score against the tight seam bowling of McKenzie, Hawke and Corling.

I had a spot of luck at 25 when a ball jumped to the shoulder of my bat, slapped me in the jaw, and floated over the head of gully. Fortunately for me Peter Burge couldn't get to it in time, though it seemed to hang in the air like a balloon.

When several balls kicked up off a length, I began to wonder if the notorious Lord's 'ridge' of 1961 was still there.

During the partnership, Peter and I ran like hares, stealing singles and turning twos into threes. After Peter was l.b.w. to a ball from Corling that came down the slope, Phil Sharpe and I added 55 in rotten light.

Yet there was no question of an appeal. Time was precious and we had to utilise every minute. We just had to hang on. But we couldn't establish the long partnership we needed.

Bobby Simpson, bowling his leg-breaks into a worn area, posed problems to me, though I did manage to hit him over the ropes twice.

My timing lost itself against relentlessly tight bowling during the afternoon, and many times my frustration threatened to get the better of me. Quite a few balls were a little too wide for offering a reasonable safe stroke, a point which is not always appreciated by onlookers side-on to the wicket.

Just before tea, with my score at 96, and after some watchful maiden overs, I lofted Simpson over mid-off but tantalisingly the ball stopped inches inside the boundary.

Soon, however, I square-cut Neil Hawke off the meat of the bat and the hundred was mine.

At tea I sat in an easy chair and had a cup of tea, with my

sweaty, new England cap drying out on the window ledge. After all the hard work and disappointments this was a sublime moment. A century at Lord's in my first Test against Australia. A moment to savour.

After the tea interval we met the Queen and Prince Philip, and Her Majesty remarked that I had made a lot of people happy. I knew I could number among those people, most of them unseen, the Edriches and their friends on the farms around Blofield, where the work was forgotten as they sat by their television and wireless sets.

Eventually I was caught by Ian Redpath at slip off Graham McKenzie for 120.

I came in to a standing ovation which no flesh-and-blood mortal experiencing it could forget.

By the fifth Test of the series I was dropped from the England side after missing out on the run-making in the third Test, at Leeds ('Burge's match') and again in the mammoth-scoring fourth at Manchester. Such is cricket.

In that Old Trafford Test I fielded through Bobby Simpson's $12\frac{3}{4}$-hour 311 and suffered a hasty (and rash) downfall very early in England's reply. I blame it on inexperience. If we were going to catch Australia's 656 (and prestige was all that was left to us in this match by then) there was no need for chancy shots before one's eyesight was accustomed to the conditions, but I made one and paid the penalty.

Ken Barrington made a monumental 256, Ted Dexter a patient 174, and we passed 600 as well, drawing the match and leaving Australia in possession of the Ashes.

I gave Barrington and the late Fred Price, one of the umpires, a lift back to London. Ken was very tired from batting. So, too, was Fred after five days on his feet under a warm sun. Any tiredness I felt when I got home was strictly from motoring.

# 4

# First Test

I HAVE moved ahead in my story but I should go back to my first Test match. News of my selection came when Surrey were being beaten by Nottingham at Trent Bridge in the first week of June, 1963.

Micky Stewart and I made our way to Manchester as an established county opening pair to face the rampant West Indians, who had the good luck to bat first after Frank Worrell had won the toss. With his call, he may very well have won the match, as the pitch took more and more spin as the game progressed.

We were a long time getting our turn in the middle because West Indies batted until late on the second day, making 501 before the declaration. I caught Gary Sobers for 64 from a huge, steepling drive off David Allen, though I had an uncomfortable time thinking about things as the ball hung like a satellite in the sky.

Conrad Hunte gave their innings the substance it needed with a knock of 182, and Rohan Kanhai and Worrell came along at the right moment with some positive batting.

Our task was formidable when Micky and I prepared to face Hall and Griffith for the final fifty minutes of the day. We felt as relaxed as could be expected in the circumstances; we were club-mates of long standing.

Micky took strike to Wes Hall, who came bounding in, crucifix flashing at his throat. He ran so fast I thought he would never stop, let alone deliver the ball! When news of my selection had come through, lots of people had said, 'Well done, John, and good luck. We'll be right behind you!'

I remember thinking as Wes roared towards me, 'I don't know about my supporters being behind me—I wouldn't mind having them in front of me right now!'

But neither Hall nor Griffith bowled well that evening. Here were two newcomers opening the batting after a demoralising two days in the field. An opening bowler should have concentrated on the off-stump, But we found the ball flying in all directions. So long as we kept our heads there was no reason why we should not be able to give England's innings a big send-off.

When Wes tripped up during the first over and fell flat, it eased the tension further still. Even so, after skidding along on his elbows, he showed absolutely no sign of skin abrasion. I wondered exactly what this huge man was made of!

I think I felt a composure based on a 'nothing to lose' conviction. I reasoned that it was my first Test: if I failed I should be dropped and that would be that. The world would continue to revolve, and John Hugh Edrich would be a county cricketer, full stop. That is not to say I lacked determination. Far from it. But it was a helpful philosophy which eased the pressure.

I took four boundaries off the erratic West Indian bowling that evening, and we rested at 31 without loss. But next morning I edged one from Hall to Derryck Murray, the 'keeper', and had to leave for only 20. Murray created a West Indies Test record by taking 24 wickets behind the stumps this series, and five of his catches came from my bat in six innings.

Ken Barrington went in, completing a hat-trick of Surrey batsmen at the top of England's batting order for the first time in a home Test match, but he failed, as did many others.

Only Ted Dexter and Brian Close got going, though Micky Stewart played a tenacious innings of 37, stretched over almost two hours and a half.

Lance Gibbs, with his off-breaks did the damage, and we had to follow on 296 runs in arrears—an even worse prospect than in the first innings, especially as the ball was turning.

This time Micky Stewart and I ran up 93 runs before Hunte grasped a catch at short-leg to end my innings of 38. Frank Worrell was the bowler, achieving another of those unobtrusive captain's moves that meant so much to the success of his team throughout the tour.

I could have kicked myself for getting out so near the drawing of stumps after weathering through the front-line attack. If only Micky and I could have resumed at, say, 100 for no wicket next day. But this is all supposed to be part of the charm of cricket.

England slid steadily away against Gibbs, Stewart this time being the only batsman to stay any length of time. He made 87, but we needed half a bozen innings of that kind to have had any chance.

West Indies went to the second Test, at Lords, one-up.

And the Lord's Test match was one of the tensest of my life. As I ponder on the nail-biters in which I've taken part I realise I've probably had more than my share—especially in the year 1968, beginning in the West Indies.

But this match in 1963 had all the time-honoured ingredients of the thriller serial, with the super-climax of two balls to play and the last man in. Six runs were needed for victory, and Colin Cowdrey stood at the non-striker's end with a broken arm in plaster after an earlier knock from Wes Hall.

The match began on a high note, with Conrad Hunte hitting fours off Fred Trueman's first three balls. I wasn't close enough to hear what Freddie had to say about that, but he finished with six for 100—we dismissed them for 301—and was then well satisfied.

I opened once more with Micky Stewart just before lunch on the second day and was caught behind off Griffith's first ball. An unpleasant experience indeed for me but it led to an astonishing innings from England's captain, Ted Dexter. He slaughtered the express bowling of Hall and Griffith, racing to 70 in very quick time. Ken Barrington held the other end secure for a typically solid 60, and we got to within 4 runs of the West Indies total after all.

When we had them half out again for only 104, we all felt very hopeful, but this time it was Basil Butcher's turn to steady the West Indies batting with a wonderful 133.

Mid-way through his innings I made a diving attempt catch at mid-wicket which, if it had stuck, could have swung the match. By this time my fielding was improving considerably. New, lighter boots had a lot to do with it. But the catch didn't stick, and Butcher's knock helped set us a target of 234. We started after the runs on the Monday.

I made only eight this time, and we were in early trouble again. The ball which dismissed me barely flicked my glove, and I think that by walking immediately I clarified a dubious situation. It is relatively easy to 'walk' with a hundred under one's belt but, after making 0 and 8, and with my position far from secure, it was a testing moment.

For what it is worth, I declare myself to be a 'walker'!

On the final day, when rain and bad light delayed the start till after lunch and swung the odds right round, putting much more pressure on us in view of the slow West Indies over rate, England found her man again—this time, Brian Close. He defended fearlessly against all that Hall and Griffith could hurl down at him, collecting enough bruises in four hours to last Henry Cooper a lifetime.

I'm not so sure that his 'rush' tactics were altogether the best thing he could have done. By walking down the pitch as the fast men let fly, he probably took a lot of unnecessary punishment and may even have missed scoring opportunities. But to each his own methods, and Brian Close was an all-England hero. With his dismissal our chances crumbled.

Derek Shackleton, recalled to the England side in his 39th year, was our last fit man. We all hoped, with fifteen runs needed in nineteen minutes, that 'Shack' might be smart enough to edge a few to the ropes.

But the run-flow decreased, and we came to the last over with eight still required. Two singles, then poor old 'Shack' was run out by Frank Worrell in what amounted to a middle-aged sprint race almost the length of the pitch.

We all stood glued to the spot as Colin Cowdrey walked

through almost solid tension on his way to the wicket, preparing to bat left-handed. Two balls remained. David Allen blocked the second-last. Now, as long as Wes Hall didn't bowl a no-ball, this final ball of the match could bring us victory with a six-hit, or defeat with a dismissal—even a tie should a man be run out going for the sixth run after a series of overthrows! These West Indies certainly took some frantic finishes with them wherever they went.

Few of these thoughts actually went through our minds as we watched big Wes turn at the end of his enormous run. He bounded in towards Allen, and the crowd exploded as the ball was played safely down. The match was drawn. Our pulses began the slow descent to normal. Thoughts turned to the third Test.

And I was understandably left out of the side after my twin failures at Lord's.

I missed the fourth Test as well but immediately after it the West Indies played Surrey. A fifty and a not out century in that game manoeuvred me into position for a recall for the fifth Test.

Micky Stewart had to pull out with stomach trouble and I started the innings with Brian Bolus who had come into his own after joining Notts from Yorkshire.

There was quite a bit of stick to be taken at this time. Charlie Griffith hit me on the elbow with a beauty. It was an extremely painful knock and, by the time I left the field, the joint was badly swollen. Alec Bedser took me to St Thomas's Hospital. By now the arm was like a balloon and a lot of fluid had to be drawn off.

While I was away there was some discussion between umpire Sid Buller and the fielding captain, Frank Worrell. Buller was concerned about the frequency of the bouncers. As for Bolus and myself it was our job not to feel concerned. We had to get on with the job of playing them.

We put on 59 in an hour and a half of tedious over rate; then Brian was caught behind off Sobers and I followed next over against the same bowler, letting fly on the off-side.

I fell to a catch by the 'keeper again in the second innings, this time off Griffith, the season's chief destroyer, for 12.

Here, as was often pointed out, was where my vulnerability showed. The ball moving across me towards slip often found the edge of my bat. Left-handers must always receive a bigger ration of this kind of bowling, the important thing being to assess which balls to leave alone.

Within the next eighteen months, after a little analysis and a lot of work on the problem during a coaching engagement in South Africa, I reckoned to have ironed down this fault to a reasonable level. My aim became to strike more positively at the ball that runs away, and to maintain a straighter bat in doing so.

However, back in 1963 at The Oval, the West Indies found the edge of my bat twice, and a disappointing Test season (for me) came to an end. West Indies romped to a deserved victory, making it 3–1.

It had been a most difficult series in which to make one's début in Test cricket—Worrell's men were a superb all-round side, with the chief strength lying in their fast bowling spear-head. England never enjoyed the luxury of two batsmen playing long innings together. Wes or 'Big Charlie' repeatedly burst through for the break they needed. No Englishman managed a century during the entire series.

Fast bowlers hunt in pairs. It's an old cliché but a true one. Lindwall and Miller; Trueman and Statham; Hall and Griffith—all were formidable combinations. I never met the great Aussie pair in their heyday but in many ways they must have been like Statham and Trueman—the one deadly accurate, the other, flamboyant, unpredictable.

Hall must be most people's idea of a fast bowler. He has everything, a superb run-in, wonderful action and great speed. Yet Charlie Griffith has created more problems for me. You never quite know what to expect from him. He will amble along for four or five overs at medium pace. Then, all of a sudden, from the same loping strides, he will produce a fast yorker, a bouncer or a beamer.

I have found it harder to pick out Charlie than any other fast bowler I have faced. I would hate to be responsible for deciding whether he was bowling or throwing. Yet as a batsman I've never had sufficient time to tell myself: 'He's throwing this one. This one's genuine'. I concentrate on looking for the ball, not how it is being delivered.

The South Africans have produced some good quick bowlers in recent years, Adcock, Heine and Peter Pollock, being three of the best. When I first played against Pollock while on tour of South Africa with the late Ron Roberts, that fine cricket writer and tour manager extraordinary, I thought he was just another bowler—quick but erratic.

He looked an altogether different proposition—and a painful one—when he came to England in 1965, as I discovered in the Test at Lord's.

Yet I had only myself to blame for being struck on the temple—and ending up in hospital. Peter had bowled me two bouncers and I was looking for more of them. These were shrewd tactics on his part because he had conditioned me to expect bouncers instead of playing each ball on its merits. So I ducked to a ball which, if I had played normally, I would have thumped away on the off-side. At the same time I took my eye off its flight and lost it in the background of the pavilion. I paid the penalty.

John Snow of Sussex is the best of the current crop of England pace bowlers, and I don't think he has yet reached his peak.

He is not a strong lad, in the Trueman mould. He needs to conserve his energy for short, sharp bursts when he can be extremely fast. He bowled magnificently on the 1968 tour to the West Indies, and in the final Test against the Australians at The Oval the following August he achieved the breakthrough in the second innings. He did this after there had been a lot of fuss about his follow-through and the Australians had complained of it.

John is one of those people who can produce that little bit extra when he gets annoyed. Many bowlers lose their control when they get roused but not John. He seems to tighten up his direction and bowl even better.

David Brown (Warwickshire) doesn't do as much with the ball as John but he is a 100 per cent trier. He will never let you down and is capable of spectacular spells, as he showed when dismissing three West Indies batsmen in one over in the first Test at Port of Spain in January 1968.

Jeff Jones of Glamorgan, who had very good tours to Australia (1965–6) and West Indies (1968) is a far greater bowler than his county records show. It is sad that a tennis elbow condition has interfered with his game but it is little short of tragic that Glamorgan have not prepared the sort of wickets on which his considerable skill could have been exploited and allowed to develop. He bowls better overseas but it is ridiculous how often he has been left out of the Glamorgan side. With his strength and perseverence, he is much too good a bowler to be languishing in the second eleven. With another county, with wickets to suit seam bowlers, he would by now have developed into the world's front rank.

Jeff is certainly one of those bowlers who shouldn't be judged simply on figures. In Australia, in 1965–6, opponents frequently played and missed at him, probably because he was doing a shade too much with the ball. It is like a right-arm bowler to a left-handed batsmen. I play and miss a lot, and I think other left-handers do the same because of the angle of the ball coming across the body. Jeff does this to the right-handed batsmen. Both in Australia and in the West Indies, the batsmen often played at him without connecting. A cricketer needs luck just as much when bowling as batting, and Jeff is due for some. I felt certain he had Clive Lloyd caught for one behind the wicket in the Barbados Test of 1968 but the appeal was not upheld. I mention the occasion because it illustrates the sort of ill-fortune which Jeff has frequently suffered on tour.

While on the subject of bad luck, Geoff Arnold of Surrey has had his fill. I am sure he will come good at Test level if he can shake off his injury jinx. He moves the ball, bats usefully around number eight and is a good fielder. Yet I wouldn't class him as an all-rounder, as I believe Brian Close sees him. I suppose it depends on how much bowling he is required to do. If he has to bowl for fairly long spells, you cannot expect him to produce batting performances as well.

Ken Shuttleworth from Lancashire is another fast bowler of obvious potential. I know he has had some trouble with his run-up and, like Geoff, he has not been free of injury. He looks strong with genuine pace and, now that Brian Statham has retired, he should get ample opportunity to prove his talents.

England's fast bowling looks reasonably well cared for and, if reports of Alan Ward of Derby are well founded, it would seem that yet another player of great promise has emerged.

I have not yet seen Ward bowl and switching to slow bowlers neither have I any personal impression of Middlesex's Harry Latchman, of whom my good friend Fred Titmus has a very high opinion.

Latchman, diminutive effervescent coloured player, with a quite positive cockney accent, is an attacking leg spinner. Fred Titmus reckons that, if Latchman continues to improve, he will be a Test regular within two years.

Certainly the spin bowling lacks reserve strength. There is my Surrey colleague Pat Pocock, but who else? Jackie Birkenshaw has improved 100 per cent since leaving Yorkshire and I will be interested to see how he now fits into Leicestershire bowling plans now that another off-spinner and Yorkshireman, Ray Illingworth has taken over as captain.

Jackie is a seasoned player but, as slow bowlers take longer to learn their trade than do the quick men—although they stay in the game longer—he can still force his way to the top.

Young batsmen of above average ability seem as rare as young spinners. Keith Fletcher (Essex) deserves to be encouraged because he goes for his strokes. I hope very much that his unhappy Test début against the 1968 Australians won't affect his temperament for the big occasion. He should take heart from the knowledge that many others failed at the start of a Test career—and came good in the end. Kenny Barrington was one.

Dennis Amiss (Warwickshire) has already proved his ability in county cricket but he still has to show that he can bridge the gap between county and Test standards. At the moment the critics say he lacks the temperament for the top-class game. He could change their minds overnight if he gets the breaks at Test level.

When we played Lancashire I liked the purposeful play of little Harry Pilling, currently the smallest player in English county cricket. He is a gutsy type of batsman. He is nimble on his feet and gives the impression of being a real fighter when the chips are down.

Unfortunately, there appear all too few of these rising young batsmen. The player who really looks the part is Barry Richards from Hampshire. He is a handsome driver and is so quick to pick up the line of the ball that he seems to have time to select his stroke. I am sure he will make rapid progress. Alas, for English hopes, he is a South African from Natal, who has already made his mark in the Currie Cup. It says much for his technique that he has adjusted himself so soon to the variable English pitch conditions.

One point which puzzles many people, especially those from overseas, is why we don't produce more all-rounders. Australia, South Africa and the West Indies, in particular, constantly find players who are capable of performing a dual rôle. Why then, cannot we develop more of the 'bits and pieces' players from our 17 first class counties?

Not so many years ago almost every county possessed at least one all-rounder but circumstances have changed. Committees tend to look for the specialist batsman or bowler, and with, the standard of wickets not nearly as high today, there probably isn't the work for a genuine all-rounder. Let's face it, most sides field two or three seamers and a spinner. Under the revised scoring system, greater responsibility has been thrown on them to get wickets early in the match. They don't see themselves as run-getters as well. With cricket now extended to Sunday League matches, they reckon to do their share as bowler or batsman, and not both.

5

# An Indian Tour

A TOUR of India is an adventure. In 1963–4 I went there with Mike Smith's MCC side which played five Test matches—every one of them drawn—inside six weeks. The tour was spoiled by repeated bouts of sickness among the players. Cables went off daily to the folks at home telling them of the latest casualties.

The sights and spectacles of this mystical and hospitable country were breathtaking. The view of the Taj Mahal, for example, alone, is indeed worth the 5,000-mile trip.

As you step from the aeroplane and enter a land of contrasts—with poverty in one direction and fabulous treasures in another—it is like living through your school-days history lessons.

We had net practice at a number of former British Army camps. One day we watched polo matches and the next day, at a safe distance, we sat bewildered, as a snake charmer made his music and lured a cobra from a basket.

Other times we climbed into rickshaws and explored the downtown areas. On one of these trips Phil Sharpe, Jimmy Binks and I drew an enormous crowd of curious Indians who seemed to find us almost as interesting as visitors from another planet.

I started well with 150 in my second match, against a spin-loaded West Zone at Ahmedabad, putting on 237 for the second wicket with Brian Bolus and being pummelled by small boys upon reaching my hundred.

But on the plane trip across to Bombay I suddenly became very hot. I told Phil Sharpe, sitting next to me, that I didn't feel too bright, and by that evening I was reduced to lying helplessly on a bed, trying to muffle my groans.

A doctor came to Brabourne Stadium, where we were billeted. He placed a thermometer under my armpit, and said I was a hospital case. To my amazement also waiting for a cab to the same hospital were Micky Stewart, John Mortimore and Phil Sharpe!

At Breach Candy Hospital, a battalion of doctors floated into the ward after we had been waiting what seemed like hours. One of them looked at me and said 'Ah, yes, stomach trouble'. He then looked at Mortimore, who was even thinner than usual under the stress of his illness, and announced a similar diagnosis. Stewart and Sharpe fell into the same pathetic category, and we were left to recuperate more or less by natural means, with occasional intakes of pills, which the Indian medical staff could ill-afford. There was a shortage, and medicine was very expensive.

Two days passed, and I made hardly any progress. In fact several times I was convinced that I was about to die. In my delirium I bade farewell to The Oval and my Norfolk fields. I sank slowly into a cloud of Indian dust, with the wild chattering of the crowd in my ears. I was sweating, choking and swearing.

Once in a while I was given an injection until yet another medico came in and asked me to open my mouth. He looked at me in horror. 'My God! You've got a throat fungus!'

Now we had identified the major problem and I was soon on the way to recovery. Within days, I was nipping over the wall to the swimming pool, and my senses were restored sufficiently for me to listen to the boys battling through the Calcutta Test match.

John Mortimore and I took an overnight train from Bombay to Nagpur, where the weather was dreadfully hot, and we began playing cricket again.

By now Micky Stewart had returned home, unwell, and reinforcements had arrived in the persons of Colin Cowdrey and Peter Parfitt. (Peter turned out to be a financial wizard when it came to exchanging currency: he always managed to find a shoeshine boy or someone else in the back alleys who gave more than the ruling rate in rupees!)

So I shaped up for my first Test of the tour—the fourth, at New Delhi, where I had my ideas on batting swiftly revised for me by the techniques of Hanumant, Cowdrey and Pataudi. Survival is all that really matters in cricket in India. The theory is: why venture strokes when, by blocking hour after hour, you can wear the bowling to exhaustion and keep the score moving slowly but certainly?

The zaniness began at the pre-match practice. We had our warm-up (!) in hundred-degrees heat, and withdrew thankfully to the shade of the dressing rooms. We asked the attendant where the showers were, but he answered: 'Very sorry, sahib, no showers'.

'Oh well,' was our reaction, 'We'll just have a wash down. Where are the hand basins?'

'Very sorry, sahib, but there is no water!'

We asked what was going on. We were told that the Cricket Board had omitted to send the Water Board any Test match tickets, so the water supply had been cut off!

The sickness situation had become frightening by now. There was no question of selection. Before a match those who stood without swaying too violently automatically played. At one stage the MCC manager, David Clark of Kent aged 45 and with a damaged kneecap, was preparing to take his place in the Test side. We eyed each other anxiously as the hours went by; we thought it was the Plague of 1665 all over again!

Whenever we donned flannels and took the field, there was always plenty of activity to take our attention around the ground. Altogether one million people watched these tour matches. Many came as much to be among their animated colleagues as to enjoy the play. There was always tremendous enthusiasm and, when stumps were drawn, we had to squeeze our way through the crowds to our charabanc, which took us back to the hotel.

As each day's play progressed, it became hazardous to field too near the boundary, for all kinds of missiles sailed over the fence. These folk—a fair proportion of them at any rate—come just for the day out, and often it isn't very long before one group will be slinging dust-bombs at each other. The 'bombs' are paper bags filled with dust and burst whenever they hit anyone or anything. What a contrast to the quiet, unemotional English spectators!

Sometimes a bonfire dispels the boredom and, when the shower of fire-crackers and squashy fruit subsides, it's not unusual to see bricks and nails landing in the arena.

A long spike missed Barry Knight's head by the narrowest of margins, and I believe that when India, having beaten the Australians in 1959, were doing a lap of honour round the ground, Nadkarni was hit on the back of the head by a brick.

The cricket itself is almost invariably a big yawn, and these distractions serve only to accentuate it.

The game is played in a dream-like atmosphere. Batsmen creep to their fifties and hundreds, enjoying the material rewards from local wealthy supporters that these milestones bring. When English bowlers hit the pads it seldom seems to matter, though hardly a ball rises bail-high.

The fifth Test followed the same pattern as the others. We made 559 for eight, with centuries from Barry Knight, and Peter Parfitt and some Sussex gaiety from Jim Parks.

Then it was all Sardesai and Nadkarni. Bapu Nadkarni, in his two not out innings of 52 and 122 batted about eleven hours in all for his 174 runs and when I bowled a maiden over down the leg-side he had the nerve to complain! This was classic irony to me coming as it did during a nightmare of negative cricket.

At Amritsar our sightseeing continued. We removed our shoes and stepped inside the magnificent Golden Temple, where the priests chanted, and the waters outside were kept pure by the golden carp that swam lazily about. This was another good opportunity for the cine-camera fanatics.

We played safe this tour by taking a lot of our own provisions along with us. At times we ran short, and sometimes we dined with the British Trade Commissioner and various English families, often enjoying steak and kidney pudding. It was necessary to carry a sort of permit to drink alcohol in India, a document which I suppose many of us considered as important as our passports.

Most of us had grown tired of tinned ham and canned beer by the time our travels ended, but it was a thousand pities that in some quarters our 'food-lift' was taken as an insult to our hosts. It was not intended to be so. It was just that experience had proved that English stomachs did not adjust quickly to changes in diet.

During the following summer—1964—I caught sight of myself on a newsreel, and decided that my weight was on the up and up, or rather out and out. So I set about controlling my shape and became teetotal.

The last thing I want to sound is prudish or puritanical, but going teetotal made me a more capable professional. I'm convinced of this.

I thought of quitting the first class game during the winter of 1964.

My first marriage to the American tennis player, Pat Stewart, had already broken up. For us it was a great mistake to try to marry the two worlds of tennis and cricket. We realised this almost immediately.

On top of that I had lost my England Test place after scoring a century on my début against the Australians, and was passed over for the MCC tour of South Africa.

Any player is bound to be disappointed when, having set his heart on making an MCC tour, he learns he has not been chosen. In my depressed state of mind, the omission was a crowning blow. I have never been the sort of person who lets tomorrow take care of itself. I am always thinking of the future and what will happen if I get injured or lose form. I knew that, to secure a decent standard of living I had to be playing Test cricket and going on tours. I felt a failure. What was the point of carrying on as just another county player?

Of course, looking back one sees things differently. Nevertheless, I would have probably finished with cricket but for meeting Judith Cowan, an Australian girl who was to become my wife, in the autumn of 1965. Judy, a State representative fencer, keen swimmer, water skier, and a qualified theatre sister, shook me out of my depression. She made me believe that I still had a future in the game. Without her help and encouragement, who knows where I might have finished?

# 6

# Bad wickets

The picture in the paper one July day in 1965 showed me buckling up, hands moving defensively and too late towards my temple; my knees bent like rubber and my bat falling uselessly to the ground.

It was only a five-and-a-half ounce cricket ball which had hit me, but it had been propelled by South Africa's express bowler, Peter Pollock, and I had lost sight of it against the pavilion at Lord's.

As I staggered around the crease, wondering what in thunder had happened, Geoff Boycott hurried down the wicket to see what damage I had suffered. I said I was all right, but Geoff told me my temple was swelling up.

'Looks like you've got half the ball in it!' he comforted. I was helped from the field, and in the dressing room my head began to throb and my eyes went watery.

I was taken by stretcher to the St. John and St. Elizabeth Hospital around the corner from Lord's and, when I caught sight of the veiled matron, I thought for a moment I might have been approaching the Gates of St. Peter already! As the afternoon wore on, my painful head quietened down.

Back at Lord's England's chance of victory in the Test match gradually evaporated, and by the end the boys were fighting to ensure a draw.

Oddly enough that same day cousin Bill, captaining Norfolk in a Minor County match, also had to go to hospital. His trouble was a split hand sustained while fielding in the slips.

I was well looked after at the St. John & St. Elizabeth, and the injury healed quite rapidly. But the accident could hardly have happened at a more inconvenient moment.

I had found my way back to the England side earlier that summer and secured my berth with an innings of 310 against New Zealand at Leeds. There was an Australian trip coming up at the end of the year, and an all-important tilt with the West Indies the following summer. Yet here I was, flat on my back, with a shattering headache. These headaches were to continue for a long time.

That accident prompts me to talk about pitches but first let me make it clear that the pitch at Lord's on that day had nothing to do with the blow I received.

However, overseas, batsmen almost invariably can trust the bounce of the ball. If the ball is short pitched it will rise, extremely swiftly, but evenly. In England the bounce varies disconcertingly and there are few good wickets. I can think of Nottingham, Northampton and Old Trafford. Most of the rest are slow and that at Lord's can be disconcerting.

Surprisingly, on my tours abroad I have learnt more about batting than in all the coaching discussions I've ever had in England. On the hard wickets of Australia, West Indies and South Africa a batsman concentrates upon building an innings, knowing the batting surface will not betray him. The desperation that so often creeps into an innings on English wickets—caused by an intuitive feeling that your innings may be terminated unjustly by some freakish seam movement—is absent.

No matter how good the wicket, you still need to take time to assess it.

Even as recently as during the gruelling 1967–8 tour of West Indies I have been aware of improvements in my technique. That indiscreet cut—far from the body—has been placed where it belongs—among my memories. It may still re-appear once in a while, but batting on fast, true wickets has proved to me that this stroke carries an unjustified risk.

I began to have fresh thoughts on batting late in 1964, when I did a coaching stint in South Africa, as well as taking part in local club cricket out there.

There I found teenagers who batted with individual style. I thought it wiser for me to develop their strong shots even if they were a trifle irregular at times, and to discourage only the downright bad shots.

In England I think we tend to put all youngsters into a common mould. With such conformity in batmanship, we make the bowler's job easier.

Many English lads are sent to coaching classes even though their interest in the game is at a very early stage of development. That little spark of interest is often extinguished by the 'cult of the left elbow'. The fun is missing. The exuberance of the lad is shed in the locker rooms the moment they take off their school blazers.

No-one would seriously dispute that to play straight is very important, especially in defence, but the art of attack must not be neglected by the growing army of coaches.

Because most coaching sessions are conducted indoors in England, the importance of fielding is overlooked. You cannot practice outfielding, throwing or even close catching in the confinement of an indoor net.

Some of the climatic drawbacks which lie heavily on English batsmen will never be overcome. Overseas the game is naturally much quicker: the ball comes off fast from the sunbaked wickets, and even an edged stroke usually runs for four, whereas in England only a single might result. A drive that brings two runs on a green Kennington Oval outfield would be worth four almost every time in Brisbane or Durban.

We must try to reduce this source of frustration. The breed of accurate medium-pace bowlers in county cricket have things all their own way nine days out of ten.

Yet the batsman almost always carries the can for slow cricket.

The most pressing need is faster pitches. I am certain that many wickets up and down the country can be improved. We must not blame the rainfall statistics for everything!

Incidentally, while I was coaching in South Africa, I was most impressed at the liaison between schools and senior cricket. They have a magnificent Nuffield Schools system. Every cricket-conscious schoolboy wants to win a Nuffield cap, play in representative matches and go on tour with the Nuffield Schools team which visits Britain and other places. It is accepted that, if a boy is good enough to win selection for Nuffield Schools, he is in line for a Springbok cap. There is a great sense of pride in being known as a Nuffield Schoolboy.

I would like to see our school boys given similar encouragement. And a much closer link established between schools and the county clubs. For a start, I believe considerable benefit could emerge from the formation of a cricket league for 16-year-olds in each county.

In the first instance, a letter could be sent to the headmasters asking if their schools wished to participate. Then the best 30 or 40 schools in terms of cricketing achievement would play against each other. They would be watched by senior county players and coaches from the first class counties. The most promising boys could be sifted out and brought to county headquarters for special matches and further instruction. In that way you would be creating a personal relationship between schools and the county clubs.

The best of the 16-year-old league cricketers could be formed into Junior county sides which would play against similar county teams.

Far more must be done to encourage the schoolboys to come to the county grounds, give them a chance to play on the big Test grounds. Surely this is a great thrill for any youngster? The schoolboy leagues could have a championship match or something similar to finish the season on the county ground.

Too many players are being lost at the moment because of the lack of liaison between county clubs and schools. Under the present set-up, it is virtually impossible to keep a check on the brightest schoolboy prospects. The counties cannot afford to carry the staffs.

If schoolboy cricket was better planned and organised, county coaches would know where to go to study matches.

Far too much reliance is placed on schoolmasters recommending boys to the county clubs. But what do many of these schoolmasters know about the finer points of the game? My guess is that their knowledge is limited, to judge from the ability of some of the youngsters who have been sent along to The Oval by their school games master. Many of these youngsters just have no idea, bowling off the wrong foot, holding the bat incorrectly.

Usually only the very keen youngster gets into the game today, the one who takes the trouble to make all the enquiries himself, walks into the county ground asking for a trial and a chance. That is how Surrey captured Geoff Arnold and Pat Pocock.

Cricket will always have these types of youngsters in the game. I am worried by the number of 'half-chance' boys who might be slipping the net—the youngster who has ability but needs pushing by somebody else before he will make the effort to come to the county ground.

This is the type of schoolboy who is escaping at the present moment. Once he leaves school, he drifts away from cricket completely either because he is too shy or does not think he has sufficient ability. By organising schools on a league basis in each county I am certain the flow of talent into the game would be stepped up considerably.

If school leagues were organised on a national basis, they would provide an exciting source of talent to the county game. Meeting and receiving instruction from players they have admired only from a distance could surely only heighten the resolve of boys to enter county cricket.

Fielding still seems to be a neglected art in the schools. So many youngsters arrive at The Oval with only a rudimentary knowledge of how they should field.

In my early days at The Oval, under the Stuart Surridge influence, we did more fielding practice than any other county. Each morning we would practice on the catching cradles. There would also be high catching and ground fielding.

I always wear lightweight boots for fielding. It helps me to move faster. When I first began my county career I was put in the outfield but it didn't suit me. I like to be in the game all the time. You can spend a lot of time doing nothing in the 'country', whereas at my present position in the gully. I am close to the scene of action.

In England where the ball tends to come off low, you need to stand closer to the bat than is necessary overseas. How many times do you actually see the ball flying over the top? I think that some of our players are sometimes inclined to stand a yard or so too far back. Alan Knott, the Kent and England wicket-keeper, is one. He is always taking the ball round his ankles, and one has to remember that the slips are governed by the position of the wicket-keeper. I think Knotty—and the slips—could move up at least a yard.

The Australians made the mistake in 1968 of standing too deep. They missed several chances because they forgot that, in English conditions, they needed to be closer to the bat.

# 7

# Triple Ton Club

THE 'Triple Ton Club' has few members. Gary Sobers, Hanif Mohammad, Bobby Simpson and Bob Cowper, besides myself, have joined a list that was very limited until 1957.

Previously only Hutton, Hammond, Bradman and Surrey's Andy Sandham had passed 300 in a Test innings, and the general impression since the War has been that conditions would not, and should not, permit high-scoring on a par with that of 'the glorious 'thirties'.

The match at Headingley, Leeds, against New Zealand in 1965 was most important for me. With Dexter and Boycott injured, here I was, back in the England side once more for what was probably my final chance. I had to prove there and then that I was good enough for Test Cricket.

Nerves that had remained dormant all my life suddenly came alive. For almost half an hour that morning (when one of the greatest of Test openers, Herbert Sutcliffe, was honoured by the unveiling of gates at Headingley in his name) I looked in vain for a run to open my score, and the harder I tried against Motz, Taylor and Collinge the deeper into despair did I sink.

Then something just clicked. During that winter's coaching in South Africa I had been playing straight and hard against the medium-pacers, and back in England I carried on with this deliberate style of aggressive driving. Now, having found my gears, I began to meet the New Zealanders with the full face of the bat.

Ken Barrington came in at the fall of Bob Barber's wicket

at 13, and together we ran England's score up to 366 by the close of play. Kenny had pipped me to a hundred, but I rested that evening ahead of him with 194, and with our unfinished stand poised at 353.

It had been a spasmodic innings: I had quiet periods, then occasionally there seemed more chances, and I would cut loose, giving my shots all the power I could muster. Against Brian Yuile's left-arm slows and Vic Pollard's off-breaks, I really let my front-foot drives go.

I was dog-tired that night, but next day the innings was resumed, and I can't recall having any special ambitions regarding the ultimate end. We wanted more runs, so I continued as well as I could, always looking for the ball to hammer.

With only 16 added to the total, Kenny Barrington was caught at the wicket for 163 when we had made 369 in partnership, breaking a number of records on the way. We were an odd pair to be rewriting the record book—for twelve months I had not been considered good enough to play for England, while Ken had recently been sacked from Test cricket for exceptionally slow scoring in the Birmingham Test!

I passed 200. Never in my life had I been timing the ball so well. This was the innings of my career—not because it became the highest, but because I was using every shot I knew and nearly all these shots were coming off. The longer the innings went the more relaxed I became. All my inhibitions were gone.

I clubbed my way through the third century, and by mid-afternoon I was a boundary away from 300. There was no time to meditate. Dick Motz ran in and bowled, I let fly, and the ball was through the off-side for four.

A few minutes later Mike Smith declared the innings closed, and we set about dismissing the Kiwis.

Not that everyone was satisfied. 'Why wasn't Edrich allowed to break Sobers' world Test record?' Some people argued that a further half hour might have been enough for me to slip past Gary's 365.

But cricket matches are primarily for the winning, and the record shows that we won this one with only minutes to spare before the rain came down.

The South Africans came for the second half of the summer and I went to Lord's Test match feeling more like a Test cricketer than I had ever felt before. If previously I had lacked confidence, that Leeds innings had filled the gap.

But now, in my next two Test innings, I was steamrollered —leg-before for nought, then literally knocked out of the game by Peter Pollock.

It was an eventful summer.

In the autumn of 1965 I married Judith, with Ken Barrington a very cheerful best man.

Soon afterwards, I was flying out with Mike Smith's MCC team to Australia for what turned out to be a memorable tour—certainly the happiest of my career.

# 8

# Australia with Mike Smith

For most cricketers an MCC tour of Australia is the peak ambition. I was delighted to find my name in the list of players selected to make the 1965–6 Tour under Mike Smith's captaincy. We flew out in October, with my own passage labelled as a "honeymoon trip". Judy was due to join me for a short time in Australia, and at Newcastle, in New South Wales, I met my in-laws for the first time.

We arrived in Western Australia fresh from a month's rest after the English season and anxious to sample some of the sizzling Australian sun that the experienced traveller continually talks about. Instead, it poured with rain! And the weather was surprisingly cold.

However, we got stuck into business straight away with a tall score against Western Australia, at Perth, taking the match in the final breath by nine runs despite Peter ('Ned') Kelly's century in each innings. There were three declarations in this game; it was cricket at its best, with a good, fast pitch and intelligent captaincy on both sides.

The players we met were invariably good to know, and the general harmony helped us across the continent, interrupted only by the occasional little discord, such as when Bill Lawry trod on his wicket in the Victoria game but continued his innings after the umpires had failed to notice. It cost us a few additional runs, which irked when one bears in mind that the match was lost by 32.

In the Combined XI match at Perth, where there were three more declarations, I opened with Bob Barber again and hit 92 on a lively wicket. We already had a hint of the pace of

Perth wickets; the nets were like lightning, and out there in the middle Laurie Mayne, seeking a Test place, and Graham McKenzie, were zipping them through.

This demanded an adjustment in our timing and an acceptance of a barrage of bumping deliveries, especially from Mayne, who eventually had me caught at third man trying to square cut a bouncer.

I said farewell to my old colleague, Tony Lock, who was now playing for Western Australia, and we flew across the vastness of that state and South Australia, and beat South Australia at Adelaide, the Cathedral City. Then we moved further on to Melbourne.

Up in Euroa, still in Victoria, we were sorry to find the field completely flooded when we arrived for a one-day match. Here, after months or even years without rain, the skies had suddenly clouded over and broken, killing any chance of starting the cricket match these keen country folk had so looked forward to and worked for over a period of two years or so.

We stood around and chatted and signed autographs and wondered what the weather was like in England at that moment.

Judy joined me in Sydney, where I sat out a high-scoring match against New South Wales which we won by nine wickets after a really solid batting performance and promising spin success for Titmus and Allen. The match was made notable also by Doug Walters' first meeting with English bowlers. He made 129.

Most of us were in the runs by now. Barber, Russell, Parks, Boycott, Barrington, Smith, Titmus and myself had all approached or passed 100 by the time we braced ourselves for the first Test, in Brisbane.

It is 2,000 miles from Perth to Brisbane as the crow flies—and a good deal longer the way an MCC team goes about it—and all the way we had been playing positive, exciting cricket, disproving the theory that this was a weak MCC team. We were now considered a healthy bet for the Test series.

There were four prospective opening batsmen among us,

*Above* Congratulations from the Queen—having reached his century against Australia
*Below* Edrich on-drives Vic Pollard for six during his innings of 310 not out for England *v* New Zealand, Leeds, 1965

Ken Barrington (152 not out) and John Edrich (192 not out) leave the field at the end of the first day's play, England *v* New Zealand at Leeds, 1965, with England 366 for one wicket

*Above* Against West Indies at Old Trafford, 1963: Edrich c. Hunte, b. Worrell 38

*Right* Hit by a Trueman bouncer during his first innings against the Yorkshire and England express bowler in 1959

Players *v* Gentlemen, Lord's, 1959. Back row: John Murray, Ken Barrington, Ray Illingworth, Geoff Pullar, Tom Cartwright, John Edrich. Front row: Fred Trueman, Brian Close, Dennis Brookes, Les Jackson, Gilbert Parkhouse

but the hazards of a touring party began to overtake us as we moved north for the first major encounter.

Brisbane provided another contrast for us, with its tropical vegetation and slower pace of life. English teams have had a hard time there since the war.

We were a happy, confident band upon arrival. Then the old bogey raised its head: Cowdrey and Barber fell sick, Boycott was far from one hundred per cent, and there was a query against Eric Russell's fitness after he damaged a thumb in the Queensland match.

In this I made a fairly rapid 133 in truly tropical conditions. For the first time in my life I felt ready to faint as I stood there, sweat dripping off me, waiting for the bowler to come in. 'You wait till the weather really warms up!' said the Aussies.

Eric Russell, an attractive, polished stroke maker, and I put on 201 in the first innings and 109 in the second before he retired in pain. He was included for the first Test match at Brisbane, but his wretched luck continued to dog him: he split his hand fielding, so our batting eventually lined up—Barber, Boycott, Edrich, Barrington, Smith etc., with poor Eric coming in last to see what he could do. Unhappily for us, we did not get first use of that splendid Brisbane wicket. Lawry and young Walters were in fine form and we faced a declared total of 443.

Bob Barber was soon caught off Neil Hawke, and I walked out across the unpretentious Woolloongabba ground feeling almost at home. I had just made runs here and, with only 5 runs on the board, I felt as though I was opening the innings.

The number three berth was to be mine for the series, but Geoff Boycott and Bob Barber were often to leave me sitting for hours padded up and waiting.

This sunny day in Brisbane, Boycott and I took the score to 75, but soon England were four down for 115 as Hawke, Allan and Philpott got amongst us.

Only some lusty driving by Jim Parks and a valuable 60 from Fred Titmus preserved a little decency in the scoresheet.

We followed-on 163 behind, but, by then, it was midway

through the final day and, with three of us reaching the thirties and Boycott holding an end with his usual determination, we salvaged the match.

If Bill Lawry had been given out to our appeal before he had scored, in Dave Brown's first over of the match, how different it would have been! Those of us near the wicket were convinced there was a touch of the glove as the ball flew through to Jim Parks.

We buried our disappointment and got on with the game, and happily for all, the series proceeded smoothly. Any fears of poor umpiring were soon dispelled. Colin Egar and Lou Rowan proved throughout the series to be top-class umpires, equal to any in England, where the standards are acknowledged to be thebest in the world. The only worries we had in 1965–6 revolved round Lawry's ever-broadening bat.

Bill could field, too. A swooping catch by him of a hit off Peter Philpott ended my first innings for 32.

From Brisbane we descended to the capital, Canberra, for a match against the Prime Minister's XI, made memorable by a dazzling innings of 79 by a newcomer few had heard of in December, 1965—Paul Sheahan—and by the fact that this was the last such fixture arranged by Sir Robert Menzies, who retired as Prime Minister of Australia after a great career spread over a quarter of a century.

That evening Sir Robert held a dinner for the teams, a wonderful occasion marked by friendly informality. We were each presented with signed copies of his memorial address spoken at Sir Winston Churchill's funeral and, on a lighter side, Jimmy Burke, the former Australian opening batsman, had everyone laughing as he went through his routine of impersonating Test cricketers.

Next, Smith, Brown, Jones and Co., as were sometimes known, moved through the bush to Bathurst, then Albury, then into South Australia to Mount Gambier, enjoying fishing outings and steak barbecues along the way.

These fishing trips can be thoroughly enjoyable. They can also provide many anxious moments. In Albury a fishing trip had been arranged for any of the players interested. We were told the boat could hold half a dozen with comfort.

When six arrived at the huge reservoir outside Albury, we found that it could take six only if a couple sat on the front and another couple on the cabin roof. In our half a dozen we had the two largest members of the party, 6 ft 7 in Dave Larter and 6 ft 3 in Dave Brown.

When we failed to catch any fish in the first hour, the rest of the boys decided to go swimming. Both the two Davids are strong swimmers. But everytime they plunged into the lake they left the boat rocking dangerously. The rest of us, including two cricket writers—Clive Taylor and Peter Smith—who could not swim, were hanging on spreadeagled on the deck to prevent being tipped over the side. The chap who owned the boat did not cheer me up when he said 'Don't worry, the lake is only 80 or so feet deep!'

Another time in Sydney the players were invited to go big game fishing, chasing sharks and tuna fish. No sooner had they got outside the protection of Sydney Harbour than some were asking to return to shelter. The waves were 12 feet deep, crashing over the fishing boats.

A very green and sick looking bunch of MCC players returned to the hotel that Sunday evening. Generously the Australian players offered to arrange a similar trip on the Sunday of the Fifth Test in Melbourne. Nobody took them up on their offer!

I visited a cheese factory with Jeff Jones and Jim Parks on a very hot day (!) and later we called in at a crayfish depot, finishing up with ice-cold beer, all of which proved an enormous challenge to our constitutions!

Geoff Boycott was dismissed for 99 against South Australian Country Districts and was far from amused. Nor was I too comfortable on Christmas day—by far the hottest I'd ever known—when I was supposed to play golf.

Instead, I went down to the sea and sat in it. The water was beautifully cool and restful. The water was smooth as a mill pond. The sun's rays did their stuff. I wiggled my toes and waved to Judy, swimming nearby.

Suddenly she spotted a long dark shape in the shallow

water behind me. Racing up the beach, she shrieked out to me to get out of the water, fast! She yelled that there was a large shark only a couple of feet away!

I leapt out like a madman. But the dark shape was only seaweed! Still, there was no point in taking chances, even if England did have opening batsmen to spare on this tour.

So to the massive Melbourne Cricket Ground, where the second Test was staged.

Bobby Simpson, recovered from the broken wrist which had kept him out of the first Test, made a steady 93 with Lawry, but, apart from Bob Cowper, who was snapped up by Titmus for 99, there was no real resistance to our attack, which lacked David Brown and Ken Higgs. Jeff Jones and Barry Knight did wonderfully well, with seven wickets between them.

We started well in our chase for a first innings total well in excess of Australia's 358, thanks to a dropped catch off Boycott in the first over. I went in when the first wicket fell at 98, and, when Barber was dismissed soon afterwards, Ken Barrington and I added 108 for the third wicket.

Kenny made 63 of that number and had rather more of the strike. But it was all for the cause, and I suppose in our many partnerships together I've sometimes also had more than my share of the strike. One thing I do know is that I'm the one who has to do all the calling!

Not for the first time I had trouble against Simpson's bowling. I think Bobby had two googlies—one obvious and another quite cleverly disguised. If in doubt I played down the line. I have never been in the habit of watching a spinner's hand, though the Australians seem to believe in doing so. I have a suspicion that too close a scrutiny of a bowler's fingers twenty yards away calls for much too rapid a shortening of focus as the ball approaches.

I played and missed frequently, but I have never seen the point in fussing and worrying over this. Simpson at slip and Wally Grout at the wicket got through a lot of 'oohs' and 'aahs' and arm-waving—I really set them going!—but I managed to ignore them. What peeved me was the high proportion of hard hits that went direct to fieldsmen.

My 109 took just over five hours. Colin Cowdrey made 104 and Parks and Titmus built up the total to 558, England's highest score in Australia since 1928–9. We sat on a lead of 200, scenting strong chances of victory.

However, by stumps that evening Australia were only 69 behind, for the loss of Simpson, and we knew we had a stiff time ahead on the final day.

The turning point came on that last day after Australia had crumbled to 176 for four—Peter Burge was missed rather badly at 34. He and Walters added 198 for the fifth wicket and the game was saved. Both made centuries, and we had to accept our fate with resignation.

Without any real break we moved to Sydney for the third Test. The crowds at the net practices were a sure sign that interest in the series was intense. Both earlier drawn Tests had been engrossing games.

That made the annihilation we were about to inflict on Australia all the more surprising.

As a preamble to this third Test, several of the players from both teams went on a Guinness and Oysters party cruise in Sydney harbour. Maybe I had a bad oyster, or perhaps oysters did not mix with my champagne. Anyhow I have been off oysters ever since.

Unfortunately for Australia Bobby Simpson developed chicken-pox and had to sit out the Test match—and we all watched anxiously to see if we had caught it!

Brian Booth lost the toss for Australia, allowing England first use of a good wicket that took more and more spin as the match went on. We were given a fantastic start by Barber and Boycott: they had almost a hundred up by lunch, and 234 by tea, when Geoff was out for 84.

Barber's knock was a thriller. He blazed away in all directions and had the crowd gasping at some of his powerful blows. He was well past his hundred when the opening partnership broke up through Boycott's dismissal.

Bob continued to attack, not caring in the least when his drives were lofted. His hits were hard and usually well-placed they defied interception. This sort of thing is infectious and, although I couldn't reach his tempo, I soon found my way against an attack that had already been half-tamed. Or so we thought.

In the final session of play Neil Hawke got rid of Barber for 185 with the new ball and, before the tail commenced its resistance, Barrington, Cowdrey, Smith and Brown departed with eight runs between them—a devastating spell.

On the second morning I had reached 96 by the last over before lunch, after seeing off the fast men without too much difficulty but leading a sort of double life against the spinners. I felt left-arm spinner Sincock was playable so long as I watched for the length of the ball; he turned them a lot, but he was not very accurate. Philpott was on the spot, however, and needed watching.

I went to lunch 100 not out after my second successive Test century against Australia, and England were heading towards 450. Bill, my cousin had made one of his two centuries against Australia on this Sydney ground nineteen years before. But Jack Ikin, our baggage master, had sadder memories of his last Test in Sydney in that same series. He reminded us that he had bagged a 'pair'.

Very soon after the interval I gave a return catch to Philpott, but we were not finished yet. Jeff Jones stayed with Allen, who reached 50 and carried England to 488. They had a rumbustious last-wicket stand, most frustrating for Australia.

We got Australia out for 221 after dispensing with Bill Lawry for nought and Grahame Thomas for a brilliant 51. Bob Cowper, their elegant left-hander, made a tedious sixty, but Dave Brown 'did a Hawke' on them with three wickets in an over. The follow-on was enforced.

Now the spin boys did their stuff. The Sydney wicket gave them all the encouragement they needed, and Australia were all out for 174—Titmus four for 40, Allen four for 47. We had won by an innings, and stood one-up with two to play. Our spirits soared.

# 9

# A New Zealand Problem

The fourth Test at Adelaide was a complete turnabout of the third. Lawry made his fourth century against us that tour, and Simpson signalled his return with an innings of 225. Their opening stand of 244 snapped a record or two, and passed England's first innings by three runs!

Before the match we had to settle on a policy. Should we try to sit on our one-nil lead? Or should we go for another win? It was decided to go all out for victory. The side would not be packed with batting. We would strive to maintain the pattern of bright, attacking cricket.

These lofty motives took a jolt when Bob Barber was bowled by Graham McKenzie for a duck and we were 33 for three on a damp wicket. I was taken at slip by Simpson off McKenzie who, sadly for us, was recalled at the last minute after being left out of the original team. We could hardly believe our luck when we heard over the radio that he had been dropped, but an injury to Peter Allan meant reinstatement for McKenzie, who bowled with a lot of life and frequently moved the ball sharply off the seam.

We were beginning to recover when a mix-up cost us Cowdrey's wicket. Barrington played a ball away, and a cry from wicketkeeper Wally Grout of 'Watch the one!' was mistaken by both batsmen in the heat of battle as being a call for a run.

'Garth' McKenzie finished with six for 48 that innings and probably saved the Ashes for his country. The Australian batsmen backed him up with a massive performance, and we had to go in again 275 runs behind on first innings and wilting in the heat after a long time in the field.

And what a long field it is at Adelaide! I had to chase a few drives from mid-on and mid-off while the batsmen ran four, and I wondered how the devil I could get the ball back all that way to the wicket. One consolation was that a man can throw farther in the thin atmosphere, and the muscles seem more supple.

Again in the second innings we lost three wickets quickly. The only real resistance came from Barrington (102) and Titmus (53). Perhaps second use of the wicket might have been preferable. Whatever the case, the series was level, with all to play for at Melbourne. Australia's task, as holders of the Ashes, was less formidable than ours. They could simply sit back and let us chase.

We warmed up with a good show of batting strength in the second New South Wales match, and the runs continued to flow in the decisive final Test after Barber had been run out from a muddle and Boycott had fallen to McKenzie.

Ken Barrington, batting as brilliantly as I've ever seen him, made 115, the quickest century of the series. I helped him add 178 for the third wicket and was content to play second fiddle while he was seeing the ball so well.

Doug Walters upset our hopes. He never seemed to do much with the ball, but often bowled a good width and had men reaching and edging. He took four important wickets, though Colin Cowdrey reached 79, Jim Parks hit 89 just when it was required, and once more Fred Titmus played a most useful knock.

With 485 up, we held high hopes and, when Brown bowled Simpson for four and Thomas departed with the total only 36, we probably has a finger on the Ashes.

But we received a sharp 'hands off!' from Lawry and Cowper. They put on 212, and Walters helped Cowper add 172 runs, with a wet, cricketless day intervening.

The anti-climax to this Test rubber was a disappointment all round. Bob Cowper went on to join the 'Triple Ton' Club, and Australia declared when they were 68 runs ahead with an hour and a quarter left.

Cowper had held us up for just over 12 hours. The final

75-minute period presented problems of concentration. Three wickets fell for 34 to McKenzie; but Barrington and Cowdrey saw it out, and an engrossing series had drawn to a close.

We might have won this rubber. We played almost non-stop positive cricket and we were a happy team. We were pitted against a fine Australian batting line-up, but the bowling attack was not as formidable as in some past Australian sides. Davidson and Benaud are still badly missed. It served to show what a huge task the winning of the Ashes represents.

The greenness of New Zealand was in striking contrast to the brownness we had left behind in Australia. Gone were the endless flat vistas; the rich greenery reminded us of home, and the drop in temperature was noticeable but the tension of the mammoth Australian cricket stadiums was missing.

I left Judy in Australia for those few weeks, intending to meet her on the return journey. Things did not quite go according to plan though.

We played at Wellington, then moved to Christchurch for the first Test—a game which had its moments, principally among England's players. Ken Higgs came into his own by taking four wickets for 5 on the final day, and Colin Cowdrey took his 100th catch in Test cricket. Top scorer for us was David Allen with 88.

The match also reminds me of my early days in cricket when I had ideas of becoming a wicketkeeper. In a last desperate move to win this first Test in New Zealand I took over behind the stumps—and wicketkeeper Jim Parks attempted to turn match winner with his seldom used leg breaks.

New Zealand had slumped to 32 for eight in their second innings and we looked capable of beating the clock and pulling off a dramatic victory. Then Bob Cunis joined Lancashire-born Vic Pollard and put an end to the slump.

Minutes were ticking by as Mike Smith rang all the changes possible before he tried his last card. The New

Zealanders must have wondered what had happened when I sprinted from gully to the dressing room for no apparent reason. They soon found out when I emerged a few minutes later decked out in wicketkeeper's pads and it was Jim's turn to rush from the field. We could not afford to waste time by changing pads on the field.

Mike immediately put Jim on to bowl. He managed to make a few deliveries pitch on a length and turn but the New Zealanders held out and finished on 48 for eight. It was a gamble, but one worth trying. In the previous match in Wellington both Eric Russell and Jim Parks had taken a couple of wickets between them. When an 'occasional' bowler comes on, batsmen often relax their guard a little and made a mistake.

There is no record of my wicketkeeping in the record books. As far as I recall, I do not think I spoiled Jim's wicketkeeping figures too much!

The second Test at Dunedin, an icy affair, was also drawn and the New Zealand fast bowler Gary Bartlett whose bowling action looked suspiciously like a throw, was omitted from the third Test, at Auckland, of which I saw very little.

After fielding all the first day, I awoke at half past five next morning with dreadful stomach pains. I was taken to the local hospital, which happened to be a maternity establishment, and the doctor applied a skilful scalpel to relieve me of my appendix.

So my tour ended rather suddenly. In my opinion it should have ended for all of us in mid-February in Melbourne. I believe the time has come to streamline the MCC tour to Australasia and I make this plea to those who plan the itinerary:

Reduce the length of the tour to Australia by three to four weeks and scrap the present arrangement of going to play matches in New Zealand at the end of the Australian part of the trip.

I am sure it should be possible to cut some of the up country fixtures. I know that in these backwoods of the game, a visit from an MCC team is a great occasion. Many people spend a lot of time and energy organising these 'missionary' matches and I realise they are going to be disappointed if the England players no longer visit them, but really the Australian tour is too long.

The New Zealand part of the itinerary could be added to another tour, say India. I understand that Billy Griffith, the MCC secretary, did put such a suggestion to the New Zealand Board of Control in 1966 but they turned it down.

I hope the New Zealand authorities will reconsider the proposal. With the best will in the world, many MCC players do find the New Zealand part of the Australasian tour something of an anti-climax. Most of them are tired of cricket and are ready to fly home after the fifth Test match in Australia. Instead they have to carry on for a further month.

The people in the outlying areas in Australia are wonderfully hospitable hosts as I discovered when we were out there in 1965–6. Nevertheless, for a touring party, the one day 'bun' matches can be irksome when they are sandwiched between Tests and State games. Instead of being able to relax, they have to make long and often uncomfortable journeys to fulfil these fixtures. I am sure in these days of air travel the keen cricket fans from these areas would be willing to fly to the big cities to watch a touring team.

This may seem a strange and rather harsh remark to people in England but Australians will understand my point.

Australia is such a vast country that everybody is 'plane conscious'. Making a plane journey is no more eventful to the average Australian that hopping on a bus or taking a car ride down the M1 in England. It is almost an everyday occurrence and practically as cheap.

I also thought these excursions into the second-class game on the last trip could have been better planned.

I have already given my reasons for our failure in the Fourth Test and the defeat which stopped us winning the Ashes. We batted badly but I—and the rest of the players—believe much of this was caused by the attitude of mind.

We had left Sydney full of hope and confidence after winning the Third Test. We could not wait for the Fourth Test to come along and get to grips with the Australians again.

But we were forced to wait until we made a trip to Newcastle for a three-day second-class game. Then we had to fly to Tasmania for more flag showing, playing one game against Tasmania in Launceston and another against a Combined XI, strengthened by Test players from the mainland, in Hobart.

The matches meant very little. In fact they were a chore we wanted to get out of our system as soon as possible. But this took a fortnight and, by the time we returned to the mainland, memories of Sydney had dimmed a little and the edge had gone off our game.

Tasmania is a wonderful island, very much like parts of England—we even discovered a fish and chip shop just outside Launceston—but it was too much of a holiday. Coming back to the Test atmosphere immediately after Tasmania was like returning to the office or factory on the first day following the family holiday. It takes time to settle back into the routine.

It was very similar in Jamaica on the last tour to the West Indies when riots halted the Test match. Just before the riots started England were steamrolling their way to victory. Every member of the team was keyed to fever pitch. We could not see how we could lose.

Aching limbs were ignored, bowlers were given fresh impetus and enthusiasm by the sight of wickets falling. When you are on top you do not feel the creeping exhaustion and the fielders are on their toes despite the heat.

By the time the Jamaican riots had been put down and the glass cleared from the outfield, this wonderful anticipation of victory had been swept away. We were not the same force afterwards. At the same time the break had given the West Indies side an opportunity to pull themselves together, to study their plight coldly, put down the panic which had been sweeping through the side, affecting their judgment. They were able to plan their path from disaster.

In the same way the Australians had been given a chance to pull themselves together following their huge defeat in

Sydney, while we were relaxing with the generous hospitality in Tasmania.

In any circumstances an Australian tour is an exacting, though enjoyable one. But, it lasts for six months which, for the family man, can seem never ending. By eliminating these minor games and returning straight home after the fifth Test instead of going on to New Zealand, the tour would be reduced considerably.

I thought that Mike Smith was unlucky after taking the MCC side to Australia.

When he returned he began the 1966 summer by hitting 140 off the West Indies attack in the MCC match at Lord's and was named England's skipper for the first Test at Old Trafford in June. He lost the toss, the pitch quickly turned to the advantage of the spinners and the West Indies hustled to victory by a innings with two days to spare.

Immediately he was sacked—and that was the end of Mike Smith's Test career of 47 caps. It was a harsh decision. To this day I cannot see the justification for it. After all, Mike had been considered good enough to skipper a side which very nearly brought back the Ashes. He had been widely acclaimed for the enterprising cricket his team had produced. Yet just this one Test and only a few months later he was thrown out. Surely he should have been given the captaincy for all five Tests against the West Indies? That is the way to breed confidence. How can a skipper feel completely in command when everyone knows he has only been appointed for one match or for part of a series?

Mike, unfortunately, never seemed to enjoy the confidence of the selectors. Even the previous year, he was not appointed for all six Tests against New Zealand and South Africa but only three at a time.

The paradox of it all was that Mike was liked and respected by the players. That is why the tour to Australia under him was such a happy one.

He knew the game inside out and he set a great example by his close catching. If there was any fun off the field, he was in the middle of it.

Mike certainly surprised the Australians from the moment he said he wasn't going to play for a 'miserable urn'. He had come there to entertain. The Ashes, in his mind, were not the be-all and end-all of the tour. Cricket, whether it was a Test or a Sunday afternoon game, was to be enjoyed. If we won the Ashes, so much the better, but our main intention was to play brightly and positively.

He took his family with him. Some people said he could not lead a team and look after his domestic responsibilities. But he took it all in his stride.

I remember a typical moment when we went to Newcastle in New South Wales and found all the local dignitaries waiting for us on the railway station. They shook hands and then asked: 'Where is Mike Smith, your captain, the man who led you to victory in Sydney?' 'Oh, he's over there' we replied and pointed to this tall blond figure striding up the platform, a child under each arm and carrying a pushchair. With him was his wife, armed with suitcases. The locals did not believe us at first.

Mike possessed this apparently casual, unflappable way. He could stand up and make a speech at an important function without a note. He didn't mope if he made a low score. He would just flop down in the dressing room bench seat, remove his boots, put on his sandals and exclaim with a grin: 'Well, there we are, that wasn't too good was it?' (and then forget all about it).

He accepted that his players knew something of the game. If you didn't get runs, he knew you felt bad enough about it without any strictures from him. Some skippers will order extra practice and lay down the law if the game goes wrong, but not Mike. He treated every day as a new day, every match as a fresh challenge. He had no time for recriminations, but he would certainly speak his mind if he thought anyone wasn't pulling his weight.

Naturally, like everyone else in the MCC party, he was bitterly disappointed when we lost the fourth Test at Adelaide after going one up in the third Test in Sydney. Various reasons have been given for our failure—the wrong bowling formation or that we should have played an extra batsman or bowler. Maybe we should have done but the simplest explanation of all for our defeat was that three of our batsmen—Bob Barber, Geoff Boycott and I—failed in each innings. You can't expect to win Test matches when that happens.

Mike was always conscious of players' feelings. When we experienced a bad day in the field on the first day of that opening Test against the West Indies in 1966 at Old Trafford, Mike took the whole team to a village pub for a few drinks. He didn't want people talking to the players in the team's hotel and making them feel worse about the day's play.

Mr Griffith, Jack Ikin, and physiotherapist Jack Jennings, all played considerable parts in the success of that MCC tour to Australasia.

The manager and Jack Ikin were always approachable and ready to discuss any problems. Jack Jennings is a great character, a 100 per cent sportsman and a great leg-puller. We did once get our own back on him. We 'treated' his drink during our stay in New Zealand and he finished up flat on his back. He didn't know what had happened. I think that must have been the only time he wasn't banging on our doors at eight o'clock in the morning to call us for breakfast.

# 10

# Captains

I PLAYED in only one Test against the all-conquering West Indies side of 1966 but for English fans it was the most satisfying Test of the series—that final game at The Oval.

It had been a long, hard summer for England, who were outplayed much of the time and often frustrated by Gary Sobers in one fantastic escape act after another.

For the fifth Test at The Oval, Brian Close was brought in as England's captain. That was the first shock. Conrad Hunte had a stump bashed clean out of the ground by Ken Higgs almost immediately. That was the second. Then, being five or six not out overnight, I was nudged in the ribs by my wife, Judy, about five o'clock next morning: she was experiencing early labour pains!

At the maternity hospital, I was told that I wouldn't be much use there, so I wandered off and had breakfast in a café in Whitechapel High Street.

I reached The Oval around nine o'clock, which startled the gate attendant. And at regular intervals I telephoned the hospital until it was time for me to pad up.

Fortunately my concentration settled from the moment I walked onto the field, though I did not make many runs.

After wobbly middle-order batting that had us headed for yet further disappointment, we staged a tremendous recovery. Tom Graveney and John Murray both made centuries, and then, our fast bowlers, Snow and Higgs, hit 128 for the last wicket. After being 166 for seven wickets at one stage, we finished with 527!

It was quite a time for our daughter to enter the world.

Cathryn was born that morning, about thirty hours after Mrs Edrich had roused her husband from his sound, energy-giving sleep

From the bowling viewpoint The Oval victory was a team performance, but I think the batting glory belonged almost entirely to Tom Graveney and John Murray. For once, England recovered, and did so in grand manner. I felt that we were not in the home straight until Sobers was out on the final day (caught courageously very near the bat, by Brian Close, first ball off John Snow) for this man is capable of almost anything.

The West Indies, having already won the rubber conclusively, possibly had lost their keen edge by this advanced stage of the summer; yet no side ever willingly loses a Test match.

The 1966 Oval victory was cause for a special kind of elation. For a fleeting moment England, having recently won the World Cup at football, was enjoying the best of both sporting worlds. We had beaten the world cricket champions (admittedly in one game only, though we all looked forward confidently to the 1967–8 series), and Brian Close was embarked upon a successful—if brief—period of triumph as England captain which was to bring five more victories in six Tests against India and Pakistan the next year before he was superseded by Colin Cowdrey for the West Indies tour.

And what an action-packed tour that was!

But before I move on too quickly this seems to be the appropriate point to pay a personal tribute to Brian Close who initiated the further chance for me to get back into Test cricket.

When Brian was called up to skipper in the final Test against the West Indies in 1966 it was he who pressed for my return. I had always had a fairly successful time against Yorkshire and I knew that Brian liked my approach to the game. I liked his, too, but he is Yorkshire; he is hard and he has got to have the best out of you. He expects the best and he tells you what he wants.

Before The Oval Test started morale was low because of

the drubbing the West Indies had ladled out in the previous games. Brian walked into the players room and said 'Right, I know a Test match is different from a county game but we are going to bring this down to county level. Not everybody is going to succeed but we are going to win'.

He got his message through and we knew that nothing else would be good enough. He had the ability to forget everything that had gone before, to convince us we were the best side, and that is how it proved to be.

His whole cricket attitude is that Yorkshire is the best and when he is playing for England he reckons that England have got better talent than anyone else in the world.

There is no doubt, however, that, in his relationships with authority, Brian is accident prone. Perhaps you can be too confident.

Both Mike Smith and Colin Cowdrey are more defensive captains—although Colin has changed considerably in the last couple of seasons; has become much more assured. Mike played the game as he found it at the time. In his early years as captain Colin was inclined to think 'If we lose a wicket now we will be in trouble' whereas Mike would wait until the wicket fell before he thought how it affected the position.

This is not intended to be a precise analysis of captaincy. It is not possible for anyone to know how or exactly why anyone else reacts. Neither should it be interpreted as placing one captain above the other. England has been extremely fortunate in those she has had to choose from, although I think that at times Ted Dexter must have caused some disappointment with his tactics.

He played the game the way he batted, a little light-heartedly, and appeared to captain in a similar way. Even so, what a great stroke player he is.

At Leeds in 1964 Dexter took the new ball against the Australians and Peter Burge hooked it out of sight and won the match. It was plain to see then, after three or four overs, that the fast bowlers were not going to succeed but Ted persevered with them. Burge just kept on hitting them harder and harder. The spinners had had the Aussies in trouble and

Ted surely should have brought them back much sooner before Burge took control.

Wisden records 'Booth, Cowper (in his first Test), Vievers and McKenzie all failed and so at 187 when Burge had made only 38, Trueman took the ball in the 89th over. Australia were on their knees, but in the next seven overs from Trueman and Flavell, Burge and Hawke helped themselves to 42 runs and they proceeded to add 105 for the eighth wicket in 99 minutes.'

When the new ball did not work he should have gone back to the spinners straight away.

They weren't playing the spinners very well and it lost us the ruddy game.

Ted was a little aloof, kept himself to himself. I've nothing against Ted, but he never had this thing that Mike Smith and, to a certain extent, Cowdrey has, of getting close to you. In the dressing room he was much the same as he was a player on the field. He never really gave us a plan of what he was going to do and he never brought us into anything.

We still remained a lot of individuals not a team. Sometimes Ted would speak sometimes he didn't. This was part of his make up and I think because of this he would never be a great captain. He may know a lot about the game but it didn't come out on the field. I don't think Ted could give all of himself to the game. He would probably have his innings and then come in and watch the golf or racing on television and forget about the state of the game. This is the impression I got of him. He doesn't get involved deeply in the game. I think he is a little shy. When I got him talking I found him very interesting but with him the other man has to do the approach work first.

# 11

# Sobers & Co.

THE 1967–8 MCC tour of West Indies was chock-full of thrills. Those beautiful Caribbean islands turned out to be exactly as I had imagined them: with magnificent golden beaches, clear blue sea, enchanting lagoons, thousands of palm trees.

The beginning, in many ways, was far from promising for me. I was branded a 'surprise selection' in the side, not having played for England in the last four Tests of the 1967 summer and, as I packed my bags, I had a suspicion that I would not be getting too much cricket. I foresaw myself, at best, going in at number three.

In the early matches I did nothing to dispel these thoughts. The ball came through very fast on the bone-hard Barbados wickets, and the bounce was far different from what we had experienced on English wickets a few weeks before. Added to this, the light was much brighter.

The West Indian islands are happy places. There is an almost permanent holiday atmosphere about them. Gaiety and enthusiasm abound everywhere. Almost the entire population is cricket-crazy.

In Barbados we spent some time at beautiful Sandy Lane beach, days marred only by the loss of my wedding ring in the sea. Some of the team were tossing a beach ball around, and, in trying a huge left-handed throw such as The Oval has never seen, I flung my gold ring high into the air; it plopped into the sea. I had all the MCC party diving in search of it with me. But the more we splashed around the more the sand was stirred up to cloud the crystal-clear water.

I hardly knew how to break the news when I phoned Judy in England that evening.

Barbados is crowded with American tourists, and living costs are very high. Luckily we enjoyed most of the luxuries by courtesy of friends and supporters, but the large parties of English cricket fans (whose presence meant much to our morale during the Tests) must have noticed the difference between holidaying in Blackpool and holidaying in Barbados!

Having absorbed the exhilarating new sights and sounds (especially the steel bands—I could listen to the bing-bong of those oil drums for hours) we moved on to Trinidad for the first Test.

England were given a slender chance of standing up to the world champions on their home wickets, and probably this adverse betting galvanised us to even greater efforts.

I found myself listed in the Test side after all, though I was conscious yet again of the need for me to play a resounding innings. Colin Milburn had scored a century against Trinidad Colts, but had done little else and was left out. The noise was tremendous as Geoff Boycott and I walked out to start the match.

We had heard that Hall and Griffith, the West Indian opening bowlers, were no longer as fast and furious as we had known them in 1963 and 1966. Wes Hall, for one, had suffered a leg injury.

The wicket for this Test was a little slower than the typical West Indian wicket and, sure enough, we had a bit more time to play the deliveries of these fast men, if 'time' is the word when one is talking about reflexes of a fraction of a second.

Geoff and I put on 80 for the first wicket before I was caught behind. The rest of the batting order now needed to build up a formidable score. That is exactly what they did.

Geoff Boycott went on to make 68, Colin Cowdrey, stroked 72, and Ken Barrington and Tom Graveney each made a century, Ken reaching both 50 and 100 with six-hits.

At 240 for three in their first innings, it seemed that West

Indies would steer clear of danger, but Basil D'Oliveira removed Kanhai, then Jeff Jones crashed through the tail, also dismissing Clive Lloyd, who made a powerful 118. West Indies followed on 205 in arrears, with seven hours left for play.

But rain lost us almost two hours and, as the final day dragged itself out, a draw began to seem inevitable. The bowlers kept at the job, but wickets didn't tumble as we had hoped—until, that is, Robin Hobbs, spinning away, caught-and-bowled Kanhai. That was the split in the dyke wall!

Five more wickets fell in an hour before tea: David Brown, bowled fast and straight, finding strength from somewhere and performing like an opening bowler fresh on a cool May day in England.

He had Basil Butcher and Derryck Murray leg-before and bowled Griffith all in one over, the last before tea. We took our refreshment in an atmosphere of excited anticipation.

Gary Sobers, putting himself low in the batting order as in the 1966 series, was still in, which had an ominous significance. But Wes Hall, the number ten popped up a catch right after tea, and Sobers might have been stranded without partners at last. But this critical chance went begging, and the match was drawn. Hall proved a king-sized nuisance. Dave Brown once beat him four times in an over, but he hung on.

Touring teams often grow stronger as the tour progresses, and to avoid defeat in the first Test is vital. This is probably where a touring combination is most vulnerable. There is still much acclimatisation to be done. But, so far from avoiding defeat, we had almost gone one-up. Chance number one had slipped us by.

Next morning at 5 o'clock we were on our way to Montego Bay, Jamaica, the millionaires' playground. Our aircraft developed oil-pressure difficulties on the runway, and we had to breakfast at the airport, but eventually we flew to Kingston, from where a long coach ride took us through some intriguing country to Montego Bay. The road soared 1,800 feet above sea level and wound through native villages where stalls laden with lush fruit beckoned to the dry palate.

A lot of people watched our match with Jamaica Colts, many of them sitting and standing in the trees surrounding the ground.

We returned to Kingston for the second Test, playing a match against Jamaica beforehand and recording our first win of the tour. In the second innings I was run out in a photo finish that could only just have placed J. Edrich second by a hair's breadth. Colin Cowdrey, on 99, turned a ball towards square-leg, the most difficult of all fielding positions for judging the feasibility of a run. I thought we could make it, to give him his hundred, but I had to turn back and scamper for home, and Lester King's throw to the bowler's end was a good one.

The Sabina Park wicket, at Kingston, had been relaid recently, and literally shone like a mirror after the constant rolling, and cross-rolling. But huge cracks widened in it as the match progressed.

I could have poked any of my fingers, except the enlarged left-index, down some of them! The ball sometimes kicked, sometimes shot like a Joe Davis snooker stroke. At the finish of the match someone compared it in appearance with the surface of the moon.

Before the second Test began, it seemed almost certain to be a low-scoring game. But a freak storm the night before the start, when the covers were off and the groundsman's emergency dash to the ground by taxi was too late, left the pitch surprisingly slow on the first day. After Colin Cowdrey had won yet another toss (our seventh consecutive success) we took first knock, not knowing quite what to expect from this Plasticine-like wicket.

The atmosphere tingled with tension and excitement before the start as a police band paraded round the ground, and we met the Jamaican Prime Minister, Mr Hugh Shearer, who presented each of us with a set of the new Jamaican stamps with a cricket motif on them.

A packed crowd talked and shouted as Geoff Boycott and I entered the arena which, before the match was through, was to be the stage of dramatics almost on a par with the lions and gladiators of old!

Wes Hall thundered in for the first ball but someone fired a gun or let off a fire cracker. Happily for all, Wes held on to the ball and walked back into the distance to start again. And what a run-up! Apparently he has been known to push himself off on his run from the wall beneath the commentary box on this small ground!

I took 35 minutes to get off the mark that morning, resisting the bait when Messrs. Hall and Griffith bowled wide, and ducking fairly frequently under bouncers. These we usually picked out without much difficulty against the green wall that served as a sightscreen. Soon we were through the worst and settling down nicely.

The West Indies fielding was glorious, with Clive Lloyd quite fantastic. Every run had to be earned, and sometimes a contemplated single disappeared before our very eyes as a fielder swooped on the ball and cannoned it back to the wicket-keeper. By tea I was 95 not out, Geoff having been out at 49.

After the interval, Sobers tossed up a slow, curly one. I gave it the works. But my bat chipped the ground as I swung into the ball, and Kanhai took a running catch at mid-off. I was out for 96, made in four hours and a quarter, an innings that had cost a lot of sweat.

Barrington and Cowdrey saw us through to the end of the day, keeping a safe eye on the second new ball and carrying us to 222 for two. Hope was building up again.

Colin Cowdrey reached his nineteenth century for England next day, and Ken Barrington made 63, but a useful spell of leg break/googly bowling by David Holford kept England's total down to 376. It was not a massive score, but we felt we had the fast bowlers to do the job.

None of us, however, expected John Snow to achieve such a mighty triumph. He gobbled up the cream of West Indian batting and finished with seven for 49, including Gary Sobers, leg-before first ball! Shades of The Oval Test, 1966!

Geoff Boycott reckons Snow to be the best "medium-pacer" in the country. Geoff, of course, has his tongue in his cheek when he says that (I think!). This day in Kingston, John bowled very fast, cutting the ball nastily and showing immense stamina.

West Indies were humbled for 143, and for the second time running they had to follow on.

On Monday things were going steadily well for us. We had taken five second innings wickets for 205, and West Indies were still 28 runs behind, with only Sobers and Holford left of the recognised Test batsmen.

At this point, as Basil Butcher walked off the field, having been caught by Jim Parks behind the wicket, a bottle was thrown onto the field. Others followed, and soon pandemonium broke out. I was standing at leg-slip, and remember wondering what the devil was about to happen. Apparently some of the crowd disputed the legality of the catch.

We could sense the anger which stirred that section of the crowd. It was quite frightening. Colin Cowdrey walked to the enclosure to plead with them to settle down, but it seemed hopeless. We were bemused as we walked round picking up the bottles near us; but it was obvious that this was not going to be a brief interruption.

Soon we were in the dressing room, and tear gas was being used by the police in an effort to quell the disturbance. The wind, however, was against us, and clouds of gas drifted into the dressing room and created acute discomfort.

Standing under a shower, trying to clear my throat of tear gas, I mentally chalked up yet another new experience in my cricketing life.

It is recorded that we lost 75 minutes play that afternoon, but what precious minutes they were! One moment we were cruising steadily to victory; the next we were at the centre of a bizarre demonstration such as we (apart from Cowdrey, Barrington and Graveney) had only ever read about.

When we finally took the field again the offending section of the crowd had been shepherded out of the ground, but the street outside was full of demonstrators. Those with strong arms were still reaching the field with their bottles and stones.

Our concentration had snapped completely by now, and, though the cracks in the wicket were widening hourly, our bowlers couldn't seem to land the ball on them any more.

Gary Sobers, who had narrowly escaped a 'king pair' and was dropped again early in his innings, went on to his century, adding over a hundred with his cousin, David Holford, and actually enjoying the luxury of declaring at 391 for nine.

We were set to make 159 in 155 minutes (including 75 minutes on the extra day, making up for the time lost) and we soon found ourselves in horrible trouble. Boycott was bowled and Cowdrey was leg-before, both to that amazing man, Sobers, for nought; then I was bowled by a ball from Hall which landed on a crack, and Barrington was leg-before. England were 19 for four wickets that evening when Tom Graveney's light appeal was upheld.

The following day our worst dreads began to materialise Jim Parks, after being hit in the throat, was leg-before. Then Tom Graveney was out unluckily, his sweep shot rebounding from Camacho's thigh for a dolly catch to Griffith.

Fred Titmus hung around for almost a quarter of an hour, during which time probably seven or eight overs were bowled, so urgent was the West Indies mission. Basil D'Oliveira enjoyed several crucial pieces of luck.

I can't honestly recall greater personal cricket agony than on that fateful morning, sitting with the rest of the team, helpless to do anything about the England reversal, not daring to watch most of the play, but letting the shouts and groans tell the tale to us.

What an almighty relief it was when the bails were finally lifted to signal that time was up. Dave Brown had just been bowled comprehensively, but he had delayed his downfall just long enough. At 68 for eight wickets, there was not enough time for us to lose after all.

In truth, chance number two of victory had gone begging from that fateful moment when the bottles started to fly.

Bridgetown, Barbados, has the finest batting wicket (and some of the shortest boundaries) in the world. Geoff Boycott verified this with an innings of 243 against Barbados between the second and third Test matches.

We had all taken the opportunity of going up to Cave Hill,

campus of the University of the West Indies, to visit Sir Frank Worrell's grave. Most of us in the party had known and respected Frank, and were glad of the chance to pay tribute to his memory under the hot West Indian sun.

By now our personnel were undergoing a reshuffle. Vice-captain Fred Titmus lost four toes from his left foot in a swimming accident and arrangements were being made for Tony Lock to join us for the last Test or two after he had finished leading Western Australia in their Sheffield Shield campaign (which they eventually won, much to Tony's noisy delight).

I had been out relaxing on another part of the island when Fred's accident occurred. He was swimming off Sandy Lane, one of the most exclusive beaches off Barbados, when he attempted to climb into a small pleasure boat. The strong current swept his legs under the boat and his left foot was caught in the single propeller situated under the middle of the boat.

I was told of the accident when I returned to the team's hotel. It was a dreadful shock. It left the whole team stunned. It could have had a demoralising effect on the whole party but for Fred's cheerfulness. He was remarkable.

A group of us went to the hospital to visit him. We had no idea of what to expect. We certainly did not expect to see Fred sitting up in bed with a smile on his face.

'How do you feel?' somebody asked.

'Lighter' he replied.

Nothing has changed Fred. It lifted the spirits of the rest of the party and it was a wonderful sight to see him walking into the hotel only a week later just before the start of the Barbados Test match. He made a wonderful recovery.

Pat Pocock deputised for Titmus for the third Test, making his Test début at the age of 21—very young for a spin bowler in Test cricket. Yet Pat had been in first-class cricket since he was seventeen, and I think he has a fine future.

With that Bridgetown wicket awaiting us, we were sorry to lose the toss. Yet there was moisture on the wicket, and more rain fell during the day. The West Indians were very cautious. Steve Camacho was particularly slow, taking five hours to reach fifty.

Facing a total of 349, we got to the wicket just before lunch on the third day. The weather was still very hot. This time I batted for just on eight hours, after being caught behind off a Sobers no-ball before I had scored! It was an unavoidable edge too—not the result of a careless thrash after the umpire's shout. Gary must have almost choked himself, especially as Geoff Boycott and I soldiered on through a bumper barrage till the end of the day and into Monday morning before Geoff was out for 90, the total 172. It was England's first century stand for the first wicket for nineteen Test matches.

My Saturday afternoon effort was exhausting. Towards the end it was all I could do to punch the ball when it asked for it. Clive Taylor, writing for The Sun, compared me with an undernourished dwarf.

When I was caught behind off Charlie Griffith the scores were level, 349 each.

England's promising start had not led to an enormous total but Tom Graveney and Basil D'Oliveira each made yet another fifty for England, and, with John Snow, carried the score over 400. On the final day the innings closed for 449, giving us a lead of 100. But we had no time to force a result.

At one stage West Indies were 79 for three, but Butcher and Lloyd slapped the ball around, and the game ran steadily to a draw. Three no-results and two to play.

So we came to the sensational fourth Test at Port of Spain, Trinidad. Much will be written in the years to come about Gary Sobers' declaration on the last day, and most of the judgments will be passed with the benefit of hindsight. The test, to my mind, is to assess the declaration at the time it was actually made. And when it was made I, for one, was flabbergasted!

First, West Indies had dealt us much punishment in their first innings. Seymour Nurse and Rohan Kanhai hit centuries and Steve Camacho starred in a new rôle with a rapid 87. Sobers declared that innings closed at 526 for seven. We replied with 404, Colin Cowdrey getting 148.

The game was heading towards yet another stalemate on the last day. There was certainly nothing urgent about the West Indies batting, and the thoughts of most people were probably drifting already towards prospects for the fifth Test.

Then, allacazam! Forty minutes after lunch the West Indian batsmen were called in at 92 for two wickets, and we were suddenly set 215 to win in 165 minutes. Sobers was after a positive result, an attitude which warranted appreciation; but, as far as I could assess, that result was ten to one on an England victory. It seemed so much like a Gillette Cup target, and most of us had had training in this type of cricket. West Indies, however, had no bowlers to close the game up if we began to advance on our goal. They had the spinners to win the game, but no accurate fast men to shut it up tight. Hall was not playing, and Griffith was injured. It was a very sporting declaration.

We had to get a steady start. This would be our launching pad. I don't mean to create the impression that we thought the task an easy one. Seventy-eight runs per hour is an extremely rapid scoring rate in modern Test cricket, even if the bowlers do get through their overs reasonably fast (they averaged 19 overs an hour this innings).

Gary wanted three or four early wickets, and that was precisely what we intended to prevent. Geoff Boycott and I put 55 on the board, before Willie Rodriguez bowled me. The task at the tea interval had become 172 in ninety minutes, but we had nine wickets in hand, and this was the important factor in our planning.

The match was won by Cowdrey and Boycott in a stand of 118 in an hour and a quarter. I wondered what thoughts went through Gary's mind as the bowling was slaughtered. Perhaps England had been edgy at times in the past against steady wrist spin, but now there were no fears in the English camp as Cowdrey and Geoff Boycott climbed into the bowling of Gibbs, Sobers, Carew, Rodriguez and Butcher (who had astonished everyone by taking five for 34 in the first innings).

Cowdrey was caught by Sobers off Gibbs for 71, and Tom

Graveney was bowled by Gibbs almost immediately, but we had it in the bag by now. After the frustration of the first two Tests, after holding the whip-hand day in and day out during the series, we were about to achieve the thing that mattered—a definite victory. Gary Sobers had no let-out in the face of this England batting onslaught.

Basil D'Oliveira teamed up with Boycott, who finished 80 not out, and 'Dolly' made the winning hit two or three minutes from 'time'. It was all very breathtaking.

So we were one-up, and we meant to hold on to our lead. We moved across to the South American mainland for the final Test, at Georgetown, Guyana.

We lost the toss again and paid for our bad luck with many hours in the field. But, although Kanhai again reached 150, and Sobers made 152, West Indies were restricted to 414 by some courageous bowling. Jeff Jones and John Snow plugged away gamely, while Pat Pocock and Ken Barrington kept a length and found reserves of energy from somewhere.

I was out for a duck and that '0' was on the board a long time, because Boycott and Cowdrey made another long stand. They both fell at 185, Colin for 59 and Geoff for a grand 116.

We slumped rather badly after that, until Tony Lock smashed 89. Pat Pocock played a resolute part, holding an end like Godfrey Evans in 1946–7. He was 80 minutes getting off the mark!

These two added a record 109 for the ninth wicket, pulling us up by the bootlaces so that we finished only 43 in arrears.

Now West Indies went after the runs. They had to win this match, and they needed 300 runs quickly. They practically got them—264 at four an over. John Snow kept things fairly well under control, taking six for 60 off fifteen overs and finishing the series with a magnificent haul of 27 wickets in four Tests, while that BIG cricketer, Gary Sobers, was very much in the picture again with 95 not out, narrowly missing the distinction of a century in each innings.

That was the situation as we prepared for the final innings of this tremendous Test series: we needed 308 for victory.

Just before lunchtime on the final day England were swaying at 41 for five! After Lance Gibbs' off-breaks had taken four wickets with murderous swiftness, we ate our lunch in stony silence. The series, we felt, had been thrown away.

Yet, by tea time, we were all happier and talking again. The total had been built bravely to 153 without further loss. The heroes were Cowdrey and his young Kent club-mate, Alan Knott, who enjoyed an early let-off and went on defending like a Test match veteran till the end of the match.

Their stand added 127, but when Cowdrey was leg-before for 82 the spectre of defeat loomed again. Only Knott and four bowlers stood in the way of the West Indies squaring the series.

John Snow, using his long legs to advantage, stayed a long time, and we got that safe and secure feeling once more. Until he padded up once too often and the umpire's finger was raised!

The ball was keeping low now, and the crowd was stirred to excitement as it sensed local but prestige-saving victory. Tony Lock failed to repeat his first innings batsmanship, hitting a long hop down mid-off's throat, and we were wide open again. Seventeen minutes to go, Pat Pocock looking (if not feeling) jaunty as he walked to the middle. The cluster of grasping in-fielders made England's plight seem hopeless.

Knott and Pocock valiantly held on for fifteen of those minutes. Then Pat was out caught close to the bat, and last man Jeff Jones had to go out and face his fate.

I had ribbed Jeff that morning, telling him: 'If we get down to you today we'll be in a right spot!'

Now, after five gruelling Test matches that had contained so much magnificent bowling, furious batting and rapturous fielding, here at the climax, with everything depending upon him, stood Ivor Jeffrey Jones, surrounded by menacing fieldsmen, with the world's finest off-spin bowler about to bowl the final over.

Jeff prodded and poked and padded and somehow survived, and the relief at the end was tremendous. We in the dressing room were taut as full-blown balloons, and desperately glad to have the air let out.

We had beaten the world champions! Colin Cowdrey said in an interview that he felt we implanted our superiority, however marginal, during the first two days of the series, when we demonstrated that Hall and Griffith, in particular, were not going to dictate matters any longer.

Colin's whole attitude to captaincy has changed tremendously in the last couple of years. Now he is in command and he grows in stature all the time.

*Right* Edrich, aged 17, bats in a trial match at The Oval and (*below*) fourteen years later he acknowledges the applause which greeted his century against Australia in the final Test match at The Oval in 1968

A wedding in Norfolk—John and Judy Edrich with Ken Barrington (*left*) as best man

*Above* Edrich lofts a ball for six, MCC *v* Queensland 1965–6. Umpire Rowan takes evasive action

*Right* With Geoff Boycott to open the England innings against Australia, Old Trafford in 1968

Test Debut—John Edrich and Micky Stewart come out to open England's innings against West Indies at Old Trafford, 1963

12

# An Oval Victory

My chances of playing in the 1968 Test series against Australia almost went up in flames—literally!

Going into the kitchen at home, I found it filled with smoke. Across the room I could just pick out flames flickering up from the burning toast. I grabbed the tray and hurled it out through the back door.

Fortunately only the hairs on my wrist were singed, and the house escaped being turned into a raging inferno after all. I duly went up to Manchester for the first Test match, and played through a series which must rank as my best. At the end I was voted Player of the Series, and my aggregate of 554 runs in nine innings was only eight less than Denis Compton's all-time series record against Australia in England.

The 1968 season was interrupted disastrously by rain. The skies were hardly ever clear for longer than a day, and the times we had no need to unpack our bags, or had to leave the field because of rain, were beyond counting. It called for much patience. More than that, it called for a great measure of resignation.

With a late run in September, I reached 2000 runs in a season for the fourth time—very gratifying in view of the foul weather, particularly as it was my benefit year.

Among those who helped to make my benefit a great success were personalities of other spheres of entertainment. David Frost, Leslie Crowther (who is ever delighted to describe the six he hit off my bowling in a Taverners' game); Harry Secombe, bad-boy wrestler Mick McManus (who had ten stitches in a finger after fielding at Aldermaston), England footballers Johnny Haynes and Johnny Byrne, boxers Henry Cooper, Terry Spinks and Frankie Taylor.

'Z-cars' Sgt. Bert Lynch (Jimmy Ellis) drove two hundred miles to play in a match with me at Dereham in Norfolk.

This warm link between cricket and the show business world of entertainment is a pleasant thing for all who take part but it also means that through the inspiration of the Lords' Taverners, for whom Prince Philip is Twelfth Man, cricket charities have been helped by many thousands of pounds.

President of the Taverners during my Benefit Year was comedian Harry Secombe, who confesses, nay, boasts, of being an all-rounder: 'You've only got to look at my figure to see that!' He insists that the only reason he wears a cap while at a cricket match is because it has a special sharp peak 'for cutting my cheese sandwiches'. Long may his fine singing, goonery and generous friendship continue.

The Test series against Bill Lawry's Australians reached a tremendous climax at The Oval in August, but this all seemed a long way ahead back in the first week of June, when the England team gathered in Manchester for the first contest.

Compared with the team which had held out against West Indies at Georgetown in the fifth Test of the 1967–8 series, we were without Ken Barrington, David Brown and Jeff Jones, whose places were taken by Dennis Amiss, Bob Barber and Ken Higgs. We had an extra batsman, and were a fast bowler light, which made the winning of the toss more important than usual. But we lost it.

We had moments of hope. Australia were 29 for two at one stage, and, late in the afternoon, 174 for four after Lawry and Walters had each made 81. But two of the young newcomers, Paul Sheahan and Ian Chappell, put on 152, and we were chasing a first innings total of 357, respectable enough, especially as the conditions grew awkward when Geoff Boycott and I began England's reply.

The weather deteriorated and the light became poor.

McKenzie and Hawke bowled steadily, but probably too short (this has been a traditional Australian failing). Survival was far from easy and fast scoring was out of the question. Our job was to bat responsibly, and by the end of the second day we were still together with 60 on the board, our light appeal having been upheld at a quarter past five.

Of all the bowlers, Alan Connolly had seemed the one to watch most closely. He was no longer the tearaway bowler we had known in Australia. Now he bowled fast-medium, dipping the ball late, always seeming capable of moving it dangerously off the seam; he occasionally bowled a good bumper, and his slow ball was cleverly concealed.

We continued on the Saturday, and I moved on to 49. Perhaps I was about to break my Old Trafford hoodoo by reaching fifty at long last. Then Geoff cut a ball to third man. On a dry ground it would probably have been a four, but the ball slowed down in the heavy outfield and Doug Walters sprinted round to cut it off. I called for a third run, but lost valuable split-seconds as I slipped on the turn. Doug's throw was long and accurate: Barry Jarman whipped off the bails, and I was run out by inches. England: 86 for one wicket.

Half an hour later we were 97 for five! Boycott, Cowdrey, Graveney and Amiss all followed me back to the pavilion, poor Amiss halfway to his 'pair' on début against Australia—surely the most horrifying experience for any young cricketer.

We finished with 165. Bob Cowper, to his own surprise, took the bowling honours with four for 48 off 26 overs, bowling steadily enough, hardly turning the ball, but setting all the batsmen problems; the ball was not coming off the wicket at any real pace, and any attempt at lofting him over the deep-set field would almost certainly have resulted in a catch.

By the time Australia had batted again we were set a virtually impossible 413 for victory. This was our plight after batting so badly in the vital first innings. There was little we could do, outside the realms of fantasy, except to show that our first innings form was not our true form.

We went down without the usual 'last rites' of batsmen

padding and prodding and only delaying the inevitable. Basil D'Oliveira's hard-hit 87 not out was a tonic.

Any prayers for rain that may have been offered went unheeded. There was so much rain about that season, yet the skies couldn't spare even just a drop on that last day. Not that we deserved to be saved. We were outbatted, outbowled and outfielded by Australia.

Graham McKenzie, branded 'lethargic' and 'spent', yet again produced an important delivery when it mattered—a ball which flew off a length over the off-stump, catching Cowdrey's thumb and going on to Jarman. I was due to receive something similar from 'Garth' in the second Test at Lord's. You could never relax against him, and the theory that he was 'just a bowler now' had to be disregarded.

We missed the experience of Ken Barrington and, with the benefit of hindsight, we know that an extra fast bowler would have been a help, too. Yet despite all the reasoning and explanations, we were not too depressed at being one-down. We honestly felt we had the ability to come out on top as the series unfolded.

Then came the historic Lord's Test match, the much-celebrated 200th contest between England and Australia. The dinner given by MCC on the Saturday evening to mark the occasion was memorable in itself.

The guest of honour was Sir Robert Menzies, one of the greatest of cricket supporters. Bill Lawry, Australia's captain, told in his speech how Lindsay Hassett, the former Australian skipper, had stressed to him that, in ten years' time and more, people wouldn't care a damn who had won the 1968 series, but they *would* remember *how* the series had been played. And, whilst admitting that in 1961 he probably wouldn't have been able to see things this way, Bill said that both Colin Cowdrey and himself would endeavour at all times to play the type of cricket people want to see. 'Especially', he added impishly, 'now that Australia are one up!'

With a little bit of luck on our side, Australia would not still have been one up by the end of the Lord's Test. We all spent much time lamenting the bad weather which interrupted the game, but it had its moments. The very heavy rainstorm on the first day and later drizzle cut off about half the playing time from a match which England controlled practically from first to last.

On either side of the first rain interruption Colin Milburn played a wonderfully powerful innings of 83, and Geoff Boycott, receiving less acclamation, showed all his mature craftsmanship on a testing wicket with 49, often avoiding the flying ball by smart-foot and body-work, while 'Ollie' Milburn courageously, if unavoidably, copped the lot.

Ken Barrington weighed in with a solid 75, and, though the batting lacked fireworks at the end, we reached 351 for seven, a figure that offered a real chance of squeezing a follow-on when Australia batted.

The rainstorm which stopped play immediately after lunch on the first day when England were 53 for one completely flooded the ground. I had never seen anything like it, and many said that Lord's had never suffered such a torrential dousing. Those who looked closely noted a mild ridge across the wicket. The water level offered undeniable proof that the slight hump first noticed in 1961 had not, after all, been eliminated completely!

After a dreary third day—Saturday—in which only thirteen and a half overs were bowled in three spells, Colin Cowdrey declared before play began on Monday. Then came the fireworks! Australia all out 78! It isn't often that sort of headline appears. But it was not a complete surprise to us. They were an inexperienced side, and England had just the bowlers for the job on that green wicket. The persistent drizzle had slowed it down after the opening day, and several of us were convinced that, had Australia batted first, we should have got them out for even fewer.

These conditions were just where English fast-medium bowlers come into their own, and they are also just what Australian batsmen like least of all. Added to this, they had only to steer the ball a few inches above ground level this day, and English fingers clasped the catch greedily. Alan Knott was as lively and competent as ever behind the wicket, Barry Knight took a dazzling catch at gully, Colin Cowdrey held three at slip, and Tom Graveney managed an excellent catch dropping forward at second slip. *The Times* featured pictures of them all on the front page. It made a glorious sight for English eyes.

David Brown, restored to the England side, took five for 42, bowling with great hostility, and Barry Knight three for 16. Barry could so easily have had five or six wickets the way he bowled that day. He is one of the very best seam bowlers in the country. John Snow took the other wicket (Barry Jarman had to retire with a broken finger) and Derek Underwood was not even called upon.

In the follow-on Lawry and Redpath batted through one hundred minutes that evening, which left us a whole day to take ten wickets—an interesting proposition. But, almost predictably, the rains came again, and in the curtailed day's play we took four wickets for 127, and the match was drawn. There was no point in wishing and grieving. We had to start again at Edgbaston.

We felt sorry for the crowds who so often had to find their entertainment at the bars or drag off home to watch television when the rains came. For the players, there is usually plenty to occupy the time especially at Lord's. The back door of the pavilion is surrounded by friends and acquaintances anxious to chat or to have books and bats autographed. And inside the dressing rooms there are television sets and even a shove-halfpenny board.

Across in the rear building one can play squash, or even real tennis. I enjoyed a game of real tennis with Colin Cowdrey, who has such a fine eye for all ball games. On rainy days squash and real tennis are just the thing for working off frustration.

This third Test match was my first at Birmingham. In 1964 I had got no further than the door, so to speak, being omitted at the last minute when Ted Dexter proved his fitness. Now, in 1968, we didn't even reach the door on the first day. As we arrived at the ground we heard the loudspeaker announcement that hopes of play had been abandoned for the day as the ground was inches under water!

By a minor miracle the ground was fit for play next morning. The ground staff had done a great job in removing the water and drying the pitch to a playable state. It was an eloquent example of the Warwickshire Club's go-ahead attitude.

In the circumstances I felt that, when Colin Cowdrey won the toss, he should have fielded first, but the wicket, although it looked damp and might have played a little oddly, was quite slow from the start.

Whether our fast bowlers would have hoodwinked a few Australians out early on this newly-laid strip, we shall never know, but the innocence of the wicket was proved by our total of 409.

Geoff Boycott and I led off with 80, before Geoff went leg-before trying to sweep Gleeson. That brought in Colin Cowdrey for his 100th Test match. Surely it was expecting too much that he should crown the achievement with a century? Yet he did make a century, and half of it on only one good leg!

He and I added 108 for the second wicket before Eric Freeman got me through a one-handed catch by deputy wicketkeeper Brian Taber. I thought that England should have been pleased with this solid start, so essential in a five-day Test match, but there were plenty of dissatisfied critics.

The wicket may have seemed 'easy' from the Press box, and certainly it lacked the fire of the early Lord's wicket, but it is on precisely such an 'easy' wicket that strokes are most difficult to play.

Many of the critics at Edgbaston seemed to have forgotten England's five for 11 collapse at Old Trafford. Well, I hadn't!

We would all like to score a hundred in two and a half hours every time we bat but it is very, very rarely done on slow wickets, least of all in Test cricket.

Colin Cowdrey, with the aid of a runner after suffering a torn hamstring, reached his historic century after Ken Barrington had fallen leg-before for nought to Eric Freeman.

Kenny was comforted later by the news that he had received the only ball which had cut back viciously all day; and he sat waiting patiently in the pavilion a very long time before his turn came to receive it!

Someone noticed that Geoff Boycott, who was running for Cowdrey, indulged in a little piece of wishful thinking at the end of a single to Graveney: he walked in from square-leg and prepared to take his guard. Such is his love of batting!

Tom Graveney, for so long one of the world's greatest stroke-makers, made a rather subdued 96, bowled by Connolly, and we achieved the big first innings total we wanted. In England, a first innings score of around 400 puts a side decisively in the driving seat—much more so than in Tests abroad. A team seem to bowl and field better with that sort of total behind them. When you have only 250 or so on the board, the margin is so much tighter.

We had a very feasible follow-on target to aim for and, when Bill Lawry was unhappily put out of the game with a broken finger, for only six, and Ian Redpath was bowled by Dave Brown for a duck, we felt we were well on the way.

Then Bob Cowper and Ian Chappell added 111. The fortunes of the game were swaying from side to side in the very best tradition.

With only four wickets lost (plus Lawry) Australia reached 210, thus saving the follow-on; but their last five wickets fell for nine runs, and they totalled 222 after all, Derek Underwood and Ray Illingworth doing the damage.

So we needed runs quickly in the second innings, the situation contrasting greatly with that of the first, when we had the whole match ahead of us. We knew our position now, and risks were most definitely in order. We hit 142 for three wickets in roughly even time.

Australia tried to keep the game tight: only McKenzie, Freeman and Connolly were bowling—Chappell, Gleeson, Cowper and Walters were not risked. We were rather glad that McKenzie, leading Australia in Lawry's absence, didn't employ Gleeson, who would not have been easy to collar. At this stage, having seen so little of him, none of us could say with conviction that we could pick his spin. A good spinner, bowling to a well-set field, can be more difficult to score from quickly than a medium pacer. In many ways it was like the third day of some county matches.

Australia were set 330 to win at 52 an runs an hour but without Lawry, they never showed any interest in the challenge. In my opinion, they were entirely justified in this attitude. Cowper took over the Lawry role, and held Derek Underwood at bay for over after over without showing the least inclination to score runs. He was determined to keep his right-handed partners, first Redpath, then Chappell, away from Underwood's end. As a left-hander, he was in a far better position to handle Underwood's 'line' and movement.

Just before lunch on the last day, with Australia 68 for one wicket, the rain came again and, when we trooped off the field as the drizzle intensified, we were destined never to return. Three Tests gone, and Australia still sat on what might be termed an opportunist one-nil lead. Our chase had to continue at Leeds.

Headingley, Leeds, held mixed memories for me. In 1965 there had been my triple century, but in 1967, against India, whose opening attack was one of the weakest seen in post-war Test cricket, I managed to edge a ball to the wicket-keeper with only a single to my name. That was the game in which Geoff Boycott cashed in with 246 not out, Basil D'Oliveira made a century, and Ken Barrington was run out seven short of a century. Which was it to be this time?

It was to be something in between—a pair of sixties. With Cowdrey and Lawry out through injuries, their deputies tossed, and Barry Jarman called correctly for Australia. Tom Graveney led us out to field. We were not too perturbed at the prospect of fielding first, as Leeds wickets usually get better and better as the match progresses. This was to prove no exception.

BBC Sportsview cameras shot occasional scenes in the dressing room during the match, and eventually put together a fascinating television film which conveyed some of the tension inside a Test match, particularly as it affects the players themselves.

Poor Geoff Boycott, for instance, was strapped to a board after suffering a back injury in the previous Test. He was especially disappointed at having to miss this match on his home wicket.

Meanwhile, Roger Prideaux, the Northants captain, took his place at Leeds, making his Test début at the age of 29. Roger is a mature, accomplished player, and has been unlucky to have had to wait so long for his England cap. I have never known anyone so composed and calm on a Test début.

Facing an Australian total of 315 (Ian Redpath made a fine 92), Roger and I put on 123 for the first wicket before he was out, sweeping, for 64, an assured, quietly-commanding innings.

Once more England's innings fell away after a promising start, and it was left to last man, Derek Underwood, to thrash 45 not out and help us to within 13 runs of Australia. He was as pleased with those runs as if he had taken the first four wickets of the innings! Alan Connolly, bowling with plenty of variety, did the main damage with five for 72. Ted Dexter's eagerly-awaited come-back innings amounted to only ten: a typical knock from him could have put us back in that driving seat, but it was not to be.

Keith Fletcher, one of our few promising young batsmen (and a brilliant fieldsman, despite the few difficult chances that escaped him here), suffered the grim fate of a duck on his first appearance for England, and the reception given him by a small section of the Leeds crowd did nothing to make him feel any better. It was hard blooding for the youngster in front of a crowd who, besides resenting Yorkshireman Phil Sharpe's last-minute omission, felt greatly frustrated when England failed to take command of the match. They've known lots of sporting success in that part of England, and they are impatient with mediocrity.

The crowd were appeased to a certain extent by Ray Illingworth's six wickets in Australia's second innings (including three stumpings by Alan Knott) but Australia topped

300 again, with the consistent Ian Chappell making 81, and we had to score 326 for victory in 295 minutes.

The chances of reaching this target were fairly remote Being realistic about it, we knew that either Australia would have to bowl appallingly, or else two of our batsmen would have to play classic attacking innings, with luck running the right way.

When the bails were lifted for the last time we were 96 runs short, with six wickets in hand, and Keith Fletcher had reached 23 not out, partially erasing the memory of his duck.

Australia thus retained the Ashes, the greatest prize in cricket. It was something we felt would be beyond them when we had assessed our own prospects in the Spring. We had come back from West Indies brimming with confidence and sensing our opportunity of going on to beat an Australian side that had known fairly meagre success in recent seasons. We had a mature batting line-up and a young and talented all-round bowling attack. The one thing we didn't count on was the constant rain.

The Oval in August is usually a sunny place, and we looked forward to the fifth and final Test there with great hope. By squaring the series, we could at least salvage some satisfaction. We had to grab this last chance with both hands.

It was a good toss for Colin Cowdrey to win, and this time I opened England's innings with Colin Milburn. Prideaux had to drop out at the last minute, and Basil D'Oliveira was brought in, setting off a chain of events which brought much ugly publicity down on cricket, and resulted later in the cancellation of the MCC tour of South Africa at the end of 1968.

But this was all in the future as we set about our task that sunny morning. The crowd at The Oval are generally knowledgeable, and they are fair in their applause to both sides. Personally, I always sense a very reassuring support there as I pass through the members and out into the field.

I looked hard at the wicket, and had a suspicion that it had been so closely cropped that it would take a good deal of spin as the days went by. So we needed to occupy it for some while.

'Ollie' Milburn was bowled early by Connolly, and Ted Dexter batted quietly for 21 in a partnership of 56 for the second wicket; then Colin Cowdrey came in, fit again, and just as anxious as any man to level the series.

Ashley Mallett, the tall off-spinner from South Australia, came on for his first over in Test cricket, and had Cowdrey's prized wicket, leg-before for 16, with his fifth ball. Our chances of a big total were receding at 113 for three. I had now reached my fifth successive Test fifty against the Australians.

Tom Graveney proved reliable again with 63, sharing with me a vital stand of 125 for the fourth wicket, and at the end of the day, with Basil D'Oliveira in, and my own score 130 not out, England still had fair prospects of making a winning total.

First-class cricket can be very hard work at times, but moments like this make it all worthwhile. This was my fourth Test century against Australia in thirteen matches, and I had realised a cherished ambition, namely to score a Test hundred on my home ground.

When Ian Chappell bowled me next day for 164, I had made the highest score in any Test match at The Oval by a Surrey player. More important to me was the fact that it has been achieved in this crucial first innings. England were marching towards a commanding score, with D'Oliveira hitting well in an innings of 158 and Australia missing catches with amazing regularity.

We fell 6 runs short of the magic 500, but we were in that proverbial driving seat. Now we needed to run down a few Australians!

John Snow dismissed John Inverarity for a single, but Bill Lawry went on to play a characteristic innings of 135.

At one stage Australia, at 136 for one, were well on the way to meeting us on first innings, but at this point Ian Redpath was caught by Cowdrey off Snow for 67, and four more wickets fell quickly as the young Australians went for their strokes.

Ashley Mallett, with his surprisingly sound style, resisted a long time for 43 not out, and all chance of the follow-on was averted when Gleeson swept a ball away and scampered the necessary runs. Now we had a real game of cricket on our hands!

With an eventual lead of 170, we set about increasing it in a hurry. We hit the ball hard and made singles that barely seemed possible. Wickets fell fairly steadily, but we kept to schedule with 181 off 59 overs, and Australia had a day and a bit to survive. No-one had any cause to expect them to go after the 352 runs for victory, especially when Lawry and Redpath were removed for thirteen runs that Monday evening, the Australian captain to a falling catch up close by Milburn which seemed to make the ground tremble!

There must have been many English prayers that night, asking for the rain to by-pass Kennington Oval. The skies were clear on that final day of the series, and the forecast seemed innocent enough: a few showers late in the day.

Just to be sure, we needed to finish it by tea.

By lunchtime Australia had slipped to 85 for five. But a large black cloud had moved up over the gasometers, and rainspots were soon wetting our faces and arms. By the time we were in the dressing room it was raining very hard, and, the lunch interval passed, huge pools of water formed in the outfield. Many people promptly left for home, giving it up as another weather disaster.

There was no point in our feeling too upset about it. Nothing could be done. We had almost grown accustomed to having prospective victory snatched from us.

The hours slipped by, and the rain eased to a drizzle. People still talked of a probable abandonment, and it seemed only a matter of time before the official announcement.

Colin Cowdrey, in blazer and flannels, ever the optimist, tip-toed around the huge puddles and looked at the wicket. The umpires went back and forth. Someone caught sight of Bill Lawry with a wide grin.

Suddenly it became apparent that further play might be

possible. Dozens of members of the cricket public, which is supposed to be so apathetic, had joined the hard-worked ground staff in the outfield and were plunging spikes into the sodden ground to drain the water away. They did a tremendous job.

I know this Oval wicket quite well by now, and it came as no surprise to learn that the pitch itself had drained well. It should be presenting no real problems to the batsmen; it would be a pudding. We should have to use a bit of psychology.

An important factor in the recovery of the flooded ground was the dry undersoil. There had been no rain for days in London (we must have realised we were due for some more), and the thirsty ground sucked the surplus water down quite swiftly. At 4.45 p.m. we walked out behind Colin Cowdrey, needing five wickets in seventy-five minutes. It was a tall task.

And it was much, much taller when forty minutes had elapsed and still we hadn't separated Inverarity and Jarman, Australia seemed safe. We continued to crowd round the bat, and the bowlers hurried through their overs, but the ball seemed to be doing nothing unusual.

Then D'Oliveira bowled to Jarman, who played and missed. Knott, standing back, took the ball and shouted triumphantly: there was a bail on the ground. Australia's wicketkeeper had been bowled.

Mallett came in and, with his long stay of the first innings fresh in our minds, we regarded him as a very likely obstacle. Cowdrey took D'Oliveira off at the pavilion end straightaway and Underwood took over. Mallett played his first ball up to Dave Brown at short-leg, very close in, and we had another wicket.

Off the last ball of Derek Underwood's over McKenzie was caught by the same fieldsman, off bat and pad; the excitement mounted in the centre and all round the ground, where the faithful had remained and newcomers poured in as the news spread.

Johnny Gleeson tried hitting himself free of the infielders, but with so many of them he could barely find a way through. Dave Brown was hit in the stomach, but the vision of victory was so tempting that no-one fielding in that eight-yard circle was concerned with personal safety. Colin Milburn took a very painful thump on the shoulder.

Underwood changed to bowling round the wicket after a signal from Cowdrey who knows his bowling so well. To another near-hysterical outburst of cheering, Gleeson lost his off-stump.

Alan Connolly loped out, last man, with about ten minutes to go. Inverarity, the tall Western Australian, was still there, on 56, having opened the innings twenty-four hours ago.

With about five minutes left, Underwood came up from the pavilion end again. Inverarity played the first ball square to me at silly point; the next he pushed off the back foot to the bowler; to the third, he padded up—and there was a concerted appeal from all the field and many outside it. Umpire Charlie Elliott's finger went up, and we had won!

The margin was 226 runs, Underwood had seven for 50, and the series, against all the odds, had been squared. Those were the vital statistics. But to all of us the memories were not statistical, they were emotional. The expectancy of winning the Ashes, the incessant frustration, the knowledge that we were a very good side and that 1968 presented us with a heaven-sent chance to sweep right across the International cricket scene, had keyed us up to a keen pitch. At last we had something to show for it.

As a result of winning awards at Leeds and The Oval, together with a special 'Man of the Series' award, I received a cheque for £450, which went with the rest into a kitty which was split equally among the England players by our 'Saturday Club' treasurer, Geoff Boycott.

# 13

# A collector of runs

No England batsman in my time has been a greater enigma to opponents and to the cricketing public than Kenny Barrington.

When in the mood, he has been capable of pulverising the best bowling in the world. He struck 102 off 122 balls against Australia at Melbourne in 1966, which was the fastest innings of that Test series. Yet he had been dropped by England for not being bold enough!

It is easy for people on the sidelines to say he would have given English cricket far better service if he had shown more aggression. They forget that many times he has gone to the wicket when England were in a terrible mess and when he has stayed to see the team to safety. Frequently he has virtually been opening the innings, blunting the new ball and weathering all the hazards which fast bowlers produce at the start of an innings.

I was very upset to learn of his illness in Australia last winter. It seemed hard to believe that this apparently tough, dedicated cricketer who had always been so active, should go down with a heart condition. Looking back, however, I realise that something was bound to happen to him. He had worried increasingly about all manner of things connected with his cricket.

He was unhappy at the state of many of the wickets on which we had to play our matches. He told me he was getting too old to play the hook stroke, but he was still playing it as well as ever when he retired from regular play.

He would be so engrossed in staying at the crease he would

forget all about the clock. He saw his rôle as a collector of runs, even if the end product was not attractive to onlookers.

I suppose this determination to score runs, especially for England, became obsessional. Instead of going for his shots, he was inclined to push and to prod. At times he was quite willing not to go through with his stroke and to take two when he might have earned himself four. He eliminated risk in the most clinical way.

Maybe he had a too-calculated approach to batting. If he had carried on playing all his shots, he might have got a lot more fun out of the game. But, equally, he might have been a failure. Like the rest of us, he does not possess the questionable benefit of hindsight.

It should be remembered that Ken Barrington has been playing international cricket, home and abroad, for more than a decade. He has represented England around 80 times and the stresses and strains to which he has been subjected have clearly told on him. It is a great shame because Kenny, for all his introspectiveness in recent years, helped a lot of players.

I have played more than 10 years with him and no one has given me more guidance. When I scored my 300 off the New Zealanders in 1965, I was half an hour getting off the mark. I was struggling on a wicket which was giving the seamers a little encouragement early on and just couldn't get going.

Kenny could see my dilemma. He knew that shortly I would do something foolish, and throw my bat at the wrong ball. So he strolled down the wicket and murmured: 'Don't worry about scoring. If you are there at 3 o'clock you'll be around the 70 to 80 mark. Remember that. Be patient. The runs will come.

I didn't really believe him at the time, but I curbed a growing desire to have a go. Gradually the runs did come. I doubt, but for Kenny's intervention, whether I would have reached 30, let alone 300.

Kenny was very much a big match player. I have seen him going through an awful trot with Surrey but, immediately he stepped into the Test side, he would throw aside all his previous inhibitions. He had this remarkable gift for raising his game when it was most needed.

I often wonder if Kenny would have taken his batting quite so earnestly if he had been encouraged to bowl his leg breaks more frequently. It would have given him another string to his bow. Certainly, he could have become a very effective, if not top-class, leg spinner. The tragedy of English cricket in the past few years is that this type of bowler has not been employed. Even with his limited opportunities—and no bowler needs more match work than a leg spinner—Kenny picked up a lot of valuable wickets.

Kenny may appear a grim, unrelenting figure when he is batting, but in lighter moments he can be very amusing. Someone ought to record on film his W. G. Grace act. He stuffs a pillow up his shirt, dons a tiny cap, and plays strokes at the nets such as you would never dream of seeing from him in the middle.

Colin Cowdrey gives you a great sense of stability when he is batting with you. If he is going well, he can make the best bowling in the world look commonplace. Of course at times he does go into his shell, and lets the bowler dictate to him. Why he does it, I don't know. He probably doesn't know himself. Most batsmen lapse into a 'brown study' occasionally and it is always more irritating for spectators when the player happens to be such an elegant stroke maker as Colin.

Whereas Colin Cowdrey and Peter May always looked good for a century once they were set, Ted Dexter never gave one that feeling. He was an exciting player to watch when he was throwing his bat at ball. Like Peter May, he sought to impose his authority on the attack from the word go. The trouble was he did not always play as circumspectly as he might. To him the ball was there to be thrashed and often he spoiled an innings of high promise by choosing the wrong one to thrash. Still, you could appreciate his approach to the game. He was an entertainer and today more and more of the watching public demand his type of cricket.

When the England selectors brought back Ted Dexter for the Leeds Test against the Australians in 1968, people inside as well as outside the game thought they were wrong to recall someone from retirement.

Many of the players were against it. Not for the financial reasons that someone was taking away £120 Test fee from a professional player, but as a general principle.

Although I too, had misgivings, I feel the selectors were right in the special circumstances surrounding Ted's recall. Colin Cowdrey, Geoff Boycott and Colin Milburn were all missing because of injury, Tom Graveney had a split finger and Roger Prideaux and Keith Fletcher were making their Test débuts.

The alternative to having Ted Dexter was to call up another player such as Alan Jones of Glamorgan for a Test début. Going into a Test match of such importance—England had to win if we were going to take the Ashes—with three new players would have been taking too much of a risk.

Ted's experience was a safer bet. Everyone was encouraged by his double century for Sussex against Kent the Saturday before the Test in his first county championship match of the summer. As it happened, Ted did not come off at Leeds. But when we were chasing runs on the last day Ted was the only player in the England side who could have taken us to victory.

Normally I do not think any batsman who has been away from the Test scene for two or three years—with little county experience in between—can make a successful come-back. This is especially true in England where the great variety of wickets demands that a player must play regularly to keep in form.

In general I am all for building a Test squad at the start of a series and keeping them together. It helps the skipper to plan his tactics and it certainly develops team spirit.

One of the many rewards for playing Test cricket is that you get this opportunity of seeing many of the finest players in close perspective.

I always knew Tom Graveney was a magnificent stroke player but it is only when you are standing at the other end that you appreciate to the full the grace and power of his batting. He is, too, an excellent judge of a run. Tom has everything, the build, height, reach. Even the tilt of the cap carries authority!

It was said at one period in his career that Tom was no good for the big occasion. You wouldn't think it now to watch him batting. Whenever he goes to the wicket, you can almost feel the fielding side bracing themselves, as if saying to themselves: 'Now we've got a job on our hands getting rid of him'.

Tom likes to hit the ball hard and, if he has any failings, it can only be one of adjustment. Sometimes he will still be trying to penetrate the defensive field for fours when singles would keep the scoring on the move. It is the attitude of the master man who only wants the best.

The D'Oliveira Affair, as the cancellation of the MCC tour to South Africa last winter was called, put an enormous personal strain on the unwitting principal, Basil D'Oliveira, one of the nicest chaps you could wish to meet.

I heard it said (happily not by the players closest to the tour scene) that Basil could have saved all the fuss by telling MCC a year earlier that he would not be available for this tour. But why should he have pulled out? Cricket is his livelihood just like the rest of us.

We were on a tour of the West Country with the International Crusaders when the trouble blew up. 'Dolly' came round to all the England players in the party, apologising for what had happened. The response from all of us was immediate and sincere: 'Stop worrying, Bas, it's not your fault'. After all, we were grown men. We knew the score. We just felt desperately sorry that 'Dolly' couldn't realise a cherished ambition of returning to his homeland under an MCC flag.

When the anti-apartheid protestors were busy making political capital out of the tour, we did our best to keep up Basil's spirits. At tea-time we would say to him: 'You stick to the brown bread. We'll have the white'. And Basil would pretend to be offended when he was asked to share hotel room with David Brown. 'The only reason I get him is because there is no-one in the team called Black', he would say. We all refused to allow the controversy to exist between us—except in fun.

In fact, the atmosphere in the England party in recent seasons has been the best I've known. I believe it is because a lot of us came into the team around the same time—John Snow, Geoff Boycott, Jeff Jones, Ken Higgs, David Brown and Basil. You don't get the back-biting which is prevalent in some teams. No-one is blamed for mistakes. We let the game take care of itself.

14

# Opening an innings

THE great England opening partnerships of Hobbs and Sutcliffe before the last war, and Hutton and Washbrook, in the post-war period, were founded on mutual trust. They understood one another's problems. They developed an almost telepathic communication. They knew when to take the sharp single; when to exert pressure on the bowlers; when to pace their game.

Geoffrey Boycott and I try to acquire the same affinity at the wicket. We have batted a lot together in the past few years and we look upon batting as a partnership in the most literal sense of the word.

We recognise that we must be collectors of runs. We have the task of getting the side off to a good start. If we can get 80 or 90 runs for the first wicket, we have done our job. It doesn't matter to us who is the dominant partner, so long as we obtain those runs.

We don't talk in great detail beforehand about bowlers and techniques. Frankly, I think there is too much theory talked about the game. I prefer to have my mind uncluttered by what the ball might do, how I should play this stroke and that sort of thing.

But Geoff and I do our best to ease one another's batting problems. For example, after Gary Sobers had dismissed Geoff with the new ball for 90 in the first over of the second morning of the Barbados Test last year, we altered our tactics.

Until then Geoff had always taken the first delivery when we opened for England but, after this Sobers' dismissal, I always took first strike for the remainder of the series.

Geoff was worried about taking Sobers with the new ball. In the second innings of the second Test in Jamaica, Sobers had also dismissed Geoff in the first over. And Geoff recalled that Sobers had done the same thing at Nottingham during the 1966 series in England.

Sobers had boasted in Jamaica that he could get Boycott with the new ball any time he wanted. It was just kidology but Geoff was not taking any chances. He is that type of player.

He told me after that Barbados dismissal. 'Just in case Sobers is not kidding would you mind taking him. Perhaps there is something I have not quite worked out about his line of delivery seeing that he's a left hander.'

I agreed to take Gary. I argued that, if Geoff was to go quickly, it would only throw more onus on me and would be no good for the side.

Furthermore, once Geoff began thinking that Gary might castle him, he would not be playing his shots with the same assurance. The change of rôles worked well.

Somebody asked after the series was over 'why didn't Sobers pretend to open with Wes Hall or Charlie Griffith and then take the new ball himself when he saw Geoff was facing the bowler for the first ball of the match'. 'There was nothing to stop him doing this.' I replied 'And there would have been nothing to stop us swopping ends at the last moment.'

Geoff has helped me too. In the first Trinidad Test I was having difficulty against the off-spin of Lance Gibbs while he was playing him with comparative ease. In the end I said to him 'You'd better take Lance as much as you can. I'll keep away from him'.

It is the only sensible way to play. Some days you can play a particular bowler well, the next you can be in all sorts of trouble. In the Jamaica Test, Geoff was bothered by the bowling of Charlie Griffith so I stayed at Charlie's end for over after over while Geoff took on Wes Hall and Gary.

It makes it so much easier if you are batting with somebody who gives you confidence. That's why I like batting with

Boycott. He gets his head down and never, never, is anything but miserable about getting out. It makes a great difference having someone of his dedication at the other end.

Geoff or I have sometimes taken a specific fast bowler for long spells, simply because the other hasn't been sighting him well that day.

Some batsmen worry when they know a bowler is working on their known weakness. Personally it doesn't worry me. If I see that the bowler is trying to make me play the ball moving outside the off-stump, I make up my mind not to play that stroke. In any case, to lure you into playing a false shot, the bowler has to keep on dropping the ball on the right spot—and that isn't easy. It is the same hooking. If I find I am not getting the hook shot right, I cut it out of my batting for that innings. You must make up your mind either to play a particular stroke or leave well alone. It is fatal to dither. The half shot has been the downfall of so many batsmen.

Batsmen can certainly help one another enormously—something not always appreciated by spectators.

Last Summer 'Ollie' Milburn hit a dazzling 83 off the Australians at Lord's and deservedly won rave notices from the critics. But he owed a lot to 'Fiery' Boycott who took much of the bowling before rain made the pitch easier.

Geoff also kept reminding Ollie that he should keep his hook shot in cold storage until the pitch had lost some of its pace. Ollie caught the headlines the next morning but Geoff's little innings was a gem in its own right. He nursed Ollie through the most difficult period when England could easily have lost three or four wickets cheaply.

Boycott is thorough in everything he does. He likes to bat for an hour and half in the nets if he can persuade the team to stay that long! Often the other players will arrive at the ground and find him already there. Then they'll say 'Look at Fiery. He's been sleeping in his pads again' or, on the odd occasions when Geoff hasn't arrived, they'll say 'The nets can't be any good—Fiery's not here'.

Most players tend to regard a net session as a loosener, where they can try their shots and get the feel of the ball. Not so Geoff. Everything has to be right. He prepares as though about to bat in a Test Match—cap, thigh pad, the lot! Geoff believes that he can't give of his best without feeling right. Bill Lawry, the Australian skipper, is another who is keen on net practice, but in 1968 he had to be up early to beat Geoff.

Whenever they were due to meet up, Geoff would say 'I'll have to watch Bill. He'll want to bag the nets but I know who will be there first!' And so did we. Geoff never missed.

On the 1968 West Indies tour the MCC team in the West Indies made a one day visit to Tobago. It had been arranged by the Tobago and Trinidad government and Colin Cowdrey agreed that the team would give coaching tips to local schoolboys.

As the players did not have any kit with them, they gave the coaching lessons in their ordinary shirts and trousers. Not so Geoff. He disappeared and returned with borrowed cricket gear. Most of it was several sizes too big but at least Geoff had satisfied his own high standards—he was wearing white.

'Fiery' gets his leg pulled but he takes it very well. He has a sense of humour and he's never at a loss for coming back at you if you rib him. When he's got himself ready for a net work out, he'll call across the dressing room: 'Come on, then, where are my net bowlers—those easy boys, Snow and Jones' and he'll ask John Snow why he can't ever bowl above medium pace!

Boycott talks soundly about the game and can put across his case most convincingly. He maintains, for instance, that it is unnecessary to play six batsmen in a Test side. He believes that, if five batsmen can't get the runs, an additional batsmen will not make any difference. I think he has a good point. He is a very confident person, completely set on becoming a great batsman, and I would rather open an innings with him than anyone.

As a near-great player, Geoff Boycott is improving all the time. He sets himself most demanding standards and targets. He has all the shots, but he is sometimes choosy about using them. His magnificent century in the Gillette Cup Final against Surrey in 1965 will not quickly be forgotten. He showed that when he threw off the shackles he could be a brilliant stroke-maker.

Sometimes he gets bogged down. At such times his attitude is to fight his way out, without giving in to his frustration. On these occasions we can see his great strength of character. He is a collector of runs, in the best Barrington–Simpson–Hanif tradition.

Geoff stays in his room a lot when we're on tour, keeping well clear of the tropic sun! He has a sense of humour, dry variety, and a quick wit, usually demonstrated during our 'Saturday Club' meetings on tour, when we gather to exchange views and problems and jokes (and fines for not wearing the special tie or for failing to address each other as 'Mr').

These Saturday evening meetings in the West Indies often ended with Colin Milburn singing 'The Green, Green Grass of Home' (with hardly less gusto than Tom Jones), followed by other melodies whose words are best left hanging in the warm Caribbean air!

'Ollie', is one of the 'characters' of our time, and an ideal tourist. In the West Indies his cheerfulness stood a stern test—he sat on the sidelines so often, left out because of a shortage of runs from his swashbuckling bat. He is always anxious to please when batting, and in the Caribbean I don't think he was fair to himself. He tried to thump the cover off the ball far too soon. Colin Cowdrey's dictum is that if you bat carefully for half an hour it becomes a different game.

Milburn, though deadly serious about his batting, seldom gives himself this sighting period. In the West Indies he took one look at those shiny, marble-like wickets and said to himself straight away: 'Righto, you bowlers, who's going to be first into the palm trees?'

Milburn is Milburn, and nothing will change him. He is a dressing-room prankster; he is a good crooner as cricketers go; he plunges into swimming pools whenever he gets the chance floating like a hippo, blowing bubbles, jumping on people, crashing down from the high-board.

Once he dived from a height into what he thought was fairly deep water, but Robin Hobbs had been kneeling, not standing. The water was only a couple of feet deep and 'Ollie' had to be carried from the pool. They thought he must have broken both legs. But he seems really quite indestructible, like his humour.

## 15

# It is never easy

I HATE losing! So do all the Edrich cricketing family. We have always been determined to succeed. Sometimes we have struggled—and struggled painfully.

I think you must have this will-to-win if you are going to make any progress in sport. That is why Yorkshire have achieved such consistent success in the county championship. They are not content to be second best.

Too many people playing sport today—and I don't just mean cricket— do not have sufficient confidence in themselves. Yet what use is there playing competitively unless you believe you can give a good account of yourself? Once you let those nagging little doubts creep in, you are never likely to be anything more than an ordinary performer.

The trouble with some of the present-day English county players is that they don't set their sights very high. They seem content to jog along, getting their 1,200 runs or 80 odd wickets a season. They reason that they do enough to keep themselves in the job—and so they do. But can it be doing the game as a whole any good? Complacency breeds mediocrity. The danger is that the malaise will spread to youngsters entering the first-class game. They may well reason that what is good enough for the senior players is good enough for them.

How does one combat this lack of urgency, this lack of ambition? In the first place, you need a captain of drive and imagination. In the second place, you require a committee resolutely set on all the players developing a sense of pride in their team and in their own performances.

The difference one player can make to the outlook of a team can be quite remarkable.

Look what Tony Lock achieved for Leicestershire! He instilled into the team a feeling that they were as good as, if not better than, any other side in the championship. He turned them into a team of fighters. They all wanted to be in on the act.

Gary Sobers has done much the same for Nottinghamshire. He has inspired others by his own incredible feats. Stuart Surridge was another person capable of transforming players by personal example. He was not a player of great ability but people *wanted* to play for him. They respected him both as a boss and as one of themselves.

In each instance the county committee were prepared to give 100 per cent backing to their choice. The present Surrey skipper, Micky Stewart, gets the same support but I cannot help wondering whether some county committees really give their captains the backing they are entitled to expect.

We have had several cases in the past season or so of skippers resigning. I know Freddie Titmus of Middlesex was not happy at some of the performances of the younger players, and Jim Parks of Sussex also felt, rightly or wrongly, that certain members of the team were not solidly behind him.

I do not pretend to know all the circumstances of these particular examples. But, clearly, you can have only one boss. If a committee is not behind the captain, he is on an impossible wicket.

Any skipper is in an intolerable position if he wants to drop one of his senior players because he doesn't feel he is pulling his weight but is afraid to do so because of what the committee might say.

When you choose a professional from out of an existing team, he is almost certain to encounter problems. One moment he is one of the boys, the next he is their captain. I think he must establish his authority immediately he takes over. He should tell the players: 'I am captain and we are going to play it my way. If I say something must be done, I say it because I believe it is for the benefit of the team as a whole.' I accept that intention is one thing, to put it into practice quite another. Some players do take offence easily. They think they are above reproach but no captain is going to be successful as a leader unless he is completely in command.

I am against laying down a set of 'do's and don'ts' for players off the field. I think it is absurd to stipulate a curfew for grown men. They can stay out until five o'clock in the morning every day of the week, if they possess that sort of constitution, so long as the night life doesn't affect their performances on the field. The majority of players are responsible enough to realise that, if they are not fit to play, they are letting others down as well as themselves. To win matches and to earn bonus money, you need 100 per cent effort from everyone.

A skipper is everyone's hero when his team are winning. His test comes when, for a variety of reasons, the side fails to click.

Micky Stewart's task has certainly not been an easy one at The Oval in the past season or so. We have lost several good players and a number of others have been out of the team because of injury. All these factors have tended to disrupt the rhythm of the side.

But I am not pessimistic. At The Oval we have players of great promise.

Mike Edwards, who opens the batting with me now that Micky Stewart has reverted to number three, is without doubt the greatest fieldsman I have seen in the 'bat-pad' position, where he has taken many knocks and displayed great courage. In the 'suicide' position I rate him above anyone, including Brian Close.

His chief value, of course, is as a batsman. He began in first-class cricket as long ago as 1960 with Cambridge University, and in 1966 he was shifted from Surrey's middle order to open the innings. In the first four matches he and I raised 100 for the first wicket. In recent seasons he has shown his class against top bowling, taking centuries off the 1966 West Indies and the 1968 Australians.

Graham Roope is one of the most promising of the young brigade. He plays straight, and that is always a strong recommendation. In 1968 he played several vitally useful innings, fielded well at slip (or anywhere else), and proved handy as a medium-pace swing bowler. In the winter he keeps goal for Hayes football club; he lives for sport, and deserves all the success that comes his way. He is beginning to fill the gap left by Dave Gibson who, for so many seasons, performed well with bat and ball, and Dick Jefferson, who was a great loss to the county. Dick, incidentally, is taking over the captaincy of Norfolk, and together with my cousin, 'W.J.', may help to bring about a revival in Norfolk cricket.

Stewart Storey has come close to winning a place in the England side over the years. He is still only 28, and should go on improving. He is a dedicated cricketer, a great asset to Surrey as a seam bowler, slip fielder and batsman capable of a match-winning innings in the best Milburn manner. His cover-drive is an absolute boomer, but he still suffers from the occasional rush of blood, lofting the ball on the leg-side and being caught just as the crowd is settling down for some of the best in batting. In 1966 he became the first Surrey player to achieve the 'double' for 34 seasons.

Michael Hooper, the lad from Charterhouse (the school which gave us Peter May) is a tall, fair-haired batsman who was called in to play against the Australians when Ken Barrington had to withdraw with back trouble. Michael took some time to get off the mark in that innings, but finally did so with an on-drive for six into the pavilion seats. Inexperience got him out in the end. He began to hit Ashley Mallett out to long-on but the ball slightly short of a length had him hitting under it, and Bill Lawry caught him for 25. The world of cricket could hear much more of Michael.

Younis Ahmed, younger brother of Saeed Ahmed, the Pakistan Test player, has made good progress through the Surrey ranks. He seems to have overcome early hesitancy on England's softer wickets, and now bats with power and confidence. He is a left-hander capable of brilliant batting and, almost equally important, delightful fielding. We all hope he will settle into first-class cricket; he certainly seems to be moving in the right direction.

Billy Smith, another left-handed batsman, has given faithful, if spasmodic, service to Surrey for a number of years, often being called in when Micky Stewart, Ken Barrington or I have been on Test match call. He could have been a regular player with many counties, and it was good to see him receive his cap at last in 1968. Apart from playing some valuable innings, he has fielded beautifully at cover and is as safe a catch in the deep field as I have ever seen.

Turning to the bowling, it was a tragic thing that Geoff Arnold's career was interrupted by injury as it was. 'Horse' (his initials are 'G.G.') won selection for England in 1967 against Pakistan, taking five good wickets for 58 at The Oval and scoring 59 when England needed to establish a lead; this was his highest score in first-class cricket in England, and, like John Snow and Ken Higgs before him, he had chosen an important occasion on which to make it.

Jimmy Cumbes, a medium-pace bowler who came to us from Lancashire (he is also goalkeeper for Third Division football club Tranmere Rovers) took 54 wickets in 1968 at reasonable cost and proved a godsend; and Robin Jackman bowled steadily all season, taking 83 wickets.

It was a pity to see Roger Harman, the left-arm spinner, fall out of first-class cricket after such early promise. In 1964, his first full season, he took 136 wickets, and might well have gone on to emulate Tony Lock as the finest left-arm bowler in the country. But it has turned out otherwise. Now the young man carrying Surrey's hopes as a left-arm spinner is Chris Waller.

All these bowlers I have mentioned are certain of one thing at least; they will receive wholehearted support from the field, with Arnold Long (known as 'Ob' Long!), our able wicketkeeper, missing very little indeed.

Three other Test players are in our ranks at present. Pat Pocock, the optimistic young off-spinner, at the age of 22 has already been on the first-class scene for five years. I have watched his development over these seasons, and he has un-

John Edrich on his way to a fine century against Australia in the final Test at the Oval in 1968

England's captain, Colin Cowdrey, reflects on the incredibly watery Oval outfield after a violent storm had interrupted England's bid for victory over Australia on the last day of the final Test match of 1968

*Above* Australian opener Inverarity is l.b.w. to Underwood and England have beaten the Aussies—the Oval, 1968
*Below* Edrich—Man of Letters! Judy types, Cathryn watches (*Reveille Newspapers*)

doubtedly learned a lot. There is so much for a spin bowler to learn but Pat has plenty of time yet. Already he has several excellent Test match achievements to his credit.

'Percy', as we call him, is essentially a product of the 1960's—carefree without being psychaedelic—and I hope he manages to avoid losing his jauntiness in the annual hurly-burly of county cricket. He has been fortunate in one respect; after Jim Laker's retirement from the game there happened to be a need for his type of talent just at the right moment. Many a man has had to wait depressingly long for an opportunity, and a lot of players each year finally abandon hope. 'Percy' Pocock got on the merry-go-round first leap, and good luck to him!

Micky Stewart, who has led the team since 1963, is a courageous batsman and brilliant short-leg fieldsman. His eight Test caps might so easily have been many more. He is a true professional in outlook, and loves the game of cricket as dearly as any man could.

I enjoyed opening the batting with Micky. He and I got a lot of singles. We believed in tip and run as soon as we went in, especially as we were left hander and right hander. It posed the extra problems for the bowlers and kept the fielders on the move and, equally important, provided some life to the cricket.

Almost inevitably, I suppose, there are those who keep comparing the present side with the great Surrey teams of a decade ago. I wish they would sometimes stop and think that every great side must disintegrate, if only for reasons of anno domini. It needs time to rebuild.

The present Surrey players know what they have got to do: They must win something to shut up the malcontents—and that's what we aim to do. Indeed, I have two unfulfilled ambitions: to be a member of an England team which licks the Australians in a series and to help Surrey win the county title.

# 16

# Cricket transfers

In the past few years a growing number of players have become dissatisfied with their county clubs and have moved elsewhere.

Should there be more freedom, then, for players to transfer from one county to another? I don't think there is a simple answer to this question.

Most of those who have left counties in recent seasons have done so because they were unhappy at their terms of contract—wages, bonuses, contracts etc. If their requests are reasonable and no compromise formula satisfactory to both can be found, I feel a player should be free to join another club.

It does mean, too, that counties like Warwickshire and Leicestershire, which have thriving supporters' organisations, can bid for good players when they become available. A limited flow of players inside the game cannot, surely, be harmful because it helps spread the talent around the counties and stimulates interest.

In any event, I cannot foresee a free-for-all transfer system ever a practicable proposition in county cricket. There is not the money for one thing. Moreover, county cricket is only a four-months-a-year job, and a player can risk losing a lot by switching counties.

He might, for example, have to sacrifice a worthwhile winter job, and also the chance of picking up a reasonably good benefit. On top of that cricket is a way of life. The friendships built up off the field do play a part in one's attitude and performance on it. You are, after all, mixing with former players of the county, many of whom have a deep knowledge of the game. Their advice and companionship is not something you toss aside lightly.

I do not believe that county cricketers move for frivolous reasons. They know there is too much at stake—and to me it is wrong that players like Tom Graveney, who went from Gloucestershire to Worcestershire, and Barry Knight from Essex to Leicestershire should have to be lost to the game for a year or two years. The public and the game at large are the losers.

While the shortage of top class young players exists in the county game, I think that the employment of overseas players must be for the general benefit of cricket in this country.

West Indies players like Gary Sobers (Notts) and Rohan Kanhai (Warwickshire) and talented South African youngsters such as Barry Richards (Hampshire) and Mike Procter (Gloucestershire), are helping to attract more people. I certainly haven't come across any feelings of resentment from our own players. Most of them realise that they stand to gain from the introduction of these talented cricketers.

Obviously, a successful side will attract bigger crowds, membership will go up and there will be more money available for wages and bonus incentives.

Even if the present limitation on the number of overseas players which counties are permitted were to be lifted, I could never visualise a flood of players pouring in from abroad. It would cost far more than the counties could afford. Furthermore, there are not many top-class performers from overseas who could be termed box office material in England.

I am told it can cost something between £6,000 and £7,000 to bring a star player here. That includes his air fare, accommodation and the expenses of moving home. By cricket standards, that is big money, indeed. In the past I believe some of it has been paid for privately. I am not surprised, because that sort of expenditure needs some recouping—and you don't happen to sign a Gary Sobers every season!

One of cricket's many problems involves its raw material—the youngster leaving school who may have a great deal of natural ability for the game.

How can he be persuaded to join a county club when the rewards seem so frugal compared with the money to be earned in other trades and professions?

The pre-war players have told me that they earned better wages than could be obtained in many other occupations of the time. Now the whole situation has changed. Cricketers today are always being reminded that they are public entertainers. If that is true they are very much the poor relations of the entertainment business.

What is needed is for county clubs to be able to tell a lad of 16: 'Join us and we will start you off at £20 a week. You can earn £2,000 a season with us, and more than that if you reach Test status.'

Somehow the clubs have got to find ways of raising extra money to meet the mounting challenges of the 1970's. I believe the counties made a grave miscalculation when they did not capitalise on the crowds which flocked to the grounds immediately after the last war. All those spectators were ready material for the good sales promoter, the sponsor and the advertiser.

Until recently, only Warwickshire really tried to look at the professional game as big business. Because of their foresight, they now possess a magnificently equipped ground and a thriving supporters' organisation. They have even been able to give financial assistance to other counties such as Worcestershire and Essex.

Surrey are now tackling the problem on the same efficient lines. They realise of course that some of their fund raising schemes will offend the traditionalists.

When Bernie Coleman, one of the special committee charged with the task of selling the game to the public, announced that they would be selling advertising space around the ground, some people exclaimed in horror: 'It will look like a greyhound track'. Bernie's reply was to the point: 'If we don't advertise, it *will be* a greyhound track!'

Obviously, the most ingenious ways of raising money will be of no lasting avail if the counties cannot provide an attractive team. Here Nottinghamshire showed imagination when they signed Gary Sobers in 1968. He revitalised the county and gave Trent Bridge a purposeful atmosphere it had not experienced for many years.

In the long term the introduction of these stars from Australia, South Africa and the West Indies could benefit our own players. If the big names bring back the crowds, then the finances must improve and there should be more money to offer in salaries and bonuses.

No one can say that the game today lacks variety. We have five-day Tests, the Gillette Knock-out Cup competition and now the Players' County League, on Sundays.

It is good that many counties intend to take the Sunday League matches to fresh venues. It should help to kindle interest in any areas where little first-class cricket is normally seen and, incidentally, bring the local club into the public eye.

# 17

# Ashes on the shelf

THE Ashes, mythical though they are, ought to be 'placed on the shelf' at the start of a Test series and, unless won outright, left in abeyance until the next series. The final Test match on each of the last two MCC tours of Australia was marred by negative tactics. If the Ashes had to be won instead of just defended, much of that disappointment might have been avoided.

In the event of a tied series there are several ways of getting a decision, I know that in the past an extra day at the end of the series has sometimes been arranged, but I wonder if some sort of 'sudden death' play-off, as in golf, has ever been considered? It could take the form of a single-wicket contest, or a one-day match with limited overs.

The 1968 Australians were a friendly bunch of cricketers. Bill Lawry, whose injuries must have spoilt his tour more than a little, led the side very well.

Those of us who went to Australia in 1965–6 saw an awful lot of 'Phantom' Lawry; he made stacks of runs against us all over the continent. Now, on his third tour of England, and with an unusually high number of new players under his wing, he did a fine job of leadership. All his greatness came out during his innings of 135 at The Oval in the final Test—an innings of steady concentration and occasional attacking strokes as well-timed and well-placed as any in the world.

His opening partner, Ian Redpath, showed much improvement in 1968. He is a mature player now, master of his temperament and one of the fleetest-footed batsmen in the world against spin bowling. I saw a lot of him during the series when he stood close at short-leg, chewing nonchalantly between deliveries. But the strongest impression is of Redpath and Lawry as a pair—both tall, lean and angular, with their big green caps firmly on their heads, as typically Australian as any pair of down-under cricketers could be, both long-striding, unflappable, and bent on selling their wickets dearly.

Ian Chappell, grandson of the old Australian Test captain, Vic Richardson, gave great service to his side during the tour, handling the damp conditions probably better than any of his fellow-batsmen, played forward a lot and delayed his strokes. We considered him a good player in Australia, but he emerged in England as the 'find' of the series.

Doug Walters and Paul Sheahan were the centre of the advance publicity given to the Australians but neither of them scored the mountain of runs predicted. Walters did not seem able to counter the ball that moved a little. His main fault was that he didn't learn. He was playing the same way at the end of the tour.

This was the difference with Chappell. He changed his approach, adapted himself to the wickets and the conditions, and did very well. He is the player I would go for if I were in charge of a county which was looking for an overseas player.

This whole business of adjustment to different pitches is always a problem when touring.

It depends on the individual's cricketing brain. When on tour you have got to sum up the conditions and sort out the way you are going to play.

I had to do this in the West Indies last year, otherwise I would not have obtained a run. I had to cut out a lot of stroke-play outside my off-stump. I know the wickets are better out there than here and should be easier to bat on, but it is still necessary to allow time to sort things out.

Colin Milburn is great to watch once he starts doing his stuff. People will go miles to see him but how often does his type of batting come off? He does not vary his approach. Can you afford to play him in a Test side when he might only come off twice in a series? I don't think you can unless you have four or five Cowdreys or Mays in the side as well. I suppose you could play 'Ollie' if you had a good all rounder, someone of the D'Oliveira type who is stronger at batting than bowling, or a bowler like Geoff Arnold who can get a few runs so that the team then bats down to number nine. If you are playing five batters with a long tail, I don't think you can afford 'Ollie', great character that he is.

Anyway, back to the 1968 Australians. Sheahan seemed to get his foot there early and commit himself to the front foot. Mind you, he played some very good shots but it struck me that the bowler always had a chance of getting him just outside the off stump. This was probably due to lack of experience on his part.

Bob Cowper, no less than any other batsman, must have cursed the heavy 1968 rainfall. With more sun on his back, this elegant left-hander might have made many more runs. And two youngsters, John Inverarity and Les Joslin, on their first tour of England, can consider themselves unlucky that the conditions gave them precious little encouragement. We will probably hear a lot of both of them in the crucial years ahead; at present they are feeling their way carefully. It is rare for a batsman to make an immediate impression on the International scene.

Sometimes however a bowler succeeds in doing this. Johnny Gleeson is a case in point. Gleeson, with the wide grin and the 'Ken Mackay' walk, was billed as the mystery man. He had previously toured Britain with the Australian Old Collegians, but he came then as a wicketkeeper/batsman! Now, in 1968, on pitches which seldom suited him (he needs a hard, bouncing wicket), he tied us down and had us guessing at his spin. But, though we didn't always 'pick' him with confidence, he still didn't get many wickets. There was, after all, no comparison between Gleeson and the Australian terror of 1950–1, Jack Iverson.

Gleeson bowled with a flat trajectory, which partly explains our inability to use our feet to him as we probably would have done to someone slower. Most of us played him off the pitch in preference to trying to pick his spin from the hand or through the air. He was deceptive enough to escape punishment when he erred in length. All in all, he was an interesting cricketer, and became one of the personalities of the series.

To offset the decline in Neil Hawke's bowling, Australia were fortunate in having Alan Connolly, who bowled so well throughout the series. He also had to overcome recent unfitness, but there was no query against his stamina; he bowled wholeheartedly through even the longest innings, and showed us that he had learnt a lot. He varies his pace very well and moves the ball about a lot. Middlesex will be lucky, indeed, to have this gay chap on the staff in 1969. I only wish Surrey had his services. He talks cricket almost non-stop.

Reverting to Neil Hawke. I have seen so much of his bowling, both in England and in his homeland, where the hard wickets place a tremendous strain on a bowler's feet and thighs. Like most Australian bowlers, Neil probably suffered from having to bowl season after season on those wickets and he delighted in bowling in English conditions. He swung the ball quite a bit, and stayed on a nagging length. This tall, muscular man kept at us like a bloodhound.

Australia's other great fast bowler is Graham McKenzie. When the 1968 series began Graham, at the age of 26, was already a veteran with 174 Test wickets. When he took only thirteen wickets during the series many people were prepared to write him off. But I think they should hold their horses. If his tally of Test wickets dropped off, never for a moment could our concentration be relaxed, for Graham McKenzie is one of those bowlers who, even at five o'clock in the afternoon, can produce a practically unplayable ball.

I think 'Garth' would have been an even greater menace if he had had the benefit of consistent support. He is not aggressive in the Trueman manner. I would compare him with Brian Statham in his approach to bowling.

When I heard of Dave Renneberg's progress since we had been in Australia I thought he might be the new-ball partner McKenzie needed. But he could not find a place in the Test side the previous summer. Nevertheless, he could play a big part in the future of Australian cricket.

The other member of the fast bowling contingent was Eric Freeman, also a top footballer in South Australia. He came to prominence very swiftly, and must have wondered what it was all about when, only a couple of years after entering serious cricket, he was playing for Australia against England at Birmingham. He bowls a very direct line, his bumper has a surprise element about it, and he is always trying. Like another well-known footballer and trier, Nobby Stiles, Freeman wears contact lenses.

Ashley Mallett, also from South Australia and also with little first-class cricket behind him, was extremely useful as an accurate off-spinner, bowling with a very high action and turning the ball enough to keep any batsman vigilant. He was an obstinate batsman, too, with a correct style. Mallet, known as 'Rowdy' because of his quietness off the field, is another of the young brigade of whom we should see much in years ahead, even if off-spinning is rather a rare pastime in Australia.

Over the years Australia have usually had long-term wicketkeepers—Don Tallon, Gil Langley, the late Wally Grout—but this time, with burly Barry Jarman as vice-captain after a short retirement, and Brian Taber having proved very efficient in South Africa in 1966–7, the choice must have been difficult. As it happened, Jarman wore the gloves in four Tests, Taber in one. Finger injuries seemed to affect Jarman's form at times, and it will be interesting to see who keeps wicket for Australia during the next season or two. Both Jarman and Taber are fine batsmen to have at number seven.

# 18

# A World Tournament

COMPETITIVE sport has grown enormously at world level in the past few years. We have seen how such sports as Soccer, Golf, Lawn Tennis and Show Jumping have developed internationally. Why shouldn't Cricket also expand?

Let us organise an international league with a points system to be played over a five- or six-year period, to find the genuine world cricket champions.

Let us have a world cricket knock-out cup competition.

These are only a couple of suggestions. I have not worked out the practicalities but, until such ideas are put up for discussion and knocked around in committee rooms and cricketing circles all over the world, it is not possible to find out whether such a system is feasible.

Nothing should be impossible in this jet age. Distance is no longer the problem.

At the moment there is no world cricketing champion country. The title is only as unofficial one awarded by the Press. After beating Australia and England the West Indies were regarded as the champions of the world. We took the title away from them after winning in the West Indies in 1968. But there is nothing official.

Why shouldn't there be? I think one could be organised, although South Africa would have to be omitted at the present time because of her apartheid laws. Yet, who knows, the formation of such a league and knockout tournament might, in the long run, persuade her government to think again.

My suggestion is for a senior championship involving England, Australia, West Indies, Pakistan and India, and a minor competition of New Zealand, Ceylon, Canada, United States, East Africa, Holland, Denmark and Malaysia, which could also include "B" teams from England, Australia and West Indies.

A system of Test visits would have to be worked out over a five or six year span during which each country played the others once in a series. Points would be awarded for Test victories and, at the end of the allotted period, the country with most points would be the official champions of the world.

Then the system would start again with another five- or six-year plan leading up to the next world championship. I believe such an idea would lead to extra interest by the public. My suggestions may offend some of the traditionalists but, if it is to bring extra money into the game and make it financially sound, these traditionalists must give way.

As well as creating interest with the general public, such a competition may help to uplift the sport in other countries where the game has got a foothold but is not strong enough to support itself. The more countries playing cricket the better.

All these countries, big and small, could be involved in a world knock-out cup. I do not mean a one-day venture such as the Gillette Cup but a proper first-class match played until there is a definite result.

Such a draw may pair together England against Malaysia, Australia against Canada or India against Bermuda which would bring the added thrill of giant-killing acts into cricket.

To ease the financial burden, England could perhaps spend three weeks in Malaysia playing two or three other matches as well as the actual cup match. It would not be too expensive. Only 13 or perhaps 14 players would be needed for the short tour. The money raised from each cup could go into a pool to help pay the expenses of less attractive and financially-rewarding fixtures.

In time it might be possible to widen the project so that the top county of England would play the top state or island from Australia, Pakistan or the West Indies in a cup competition similar to the European Cup for soccer—Yorkshire *v* New South Wales; Surrey *v* Barbados etc.

This would create a wonderful incentive to the players in this country. It would encourage them to try and improve themselves if they could see something really worthwhile coming out of their labours. Too many cricketers seem satisfied to play for their county and nothing else. They do not try to raise their game.

# 19

# Test time

THE game of cricket is always changing. It has changed a great deal during my own career.

Among the new phenomena are the one-day Gillette Cup Matches, introduced with very high hopes, but soon subjected to cool, professional tactics which tend to squeeze the gaiety out of them. Very few committees or captains seem to believe in slow bowling in one-day cricket, and often we have to endure a stream of fast-medium bowling, with defensive fields. I am sure the original idea aimed at a brighter, more carefree approach.

Now we have the Players' County League. It will mean more travelling and less rest for county cricketers, but the rewards will be there, and the game as a whole ought to benefit. It will be, like Gillette Cup cricket, a completely different game from county cricket and, of course, even farther removed from Test match cricket. But there is room for all these variations of the game. I predict that one side-issue of the Sunday League will be that, with greater demands on the players, more cricketers from outside the first-class game will be brought into the sides on account of the strains and injuries which are likely to occur.

I regret the International Cavaliers were not invited to compete in the Players' County League. I am certain a team of former England players like Peter May, Ted Dexter, Godfrey Evans, Jim Laker, Frank Tyson, Freddie Trueman, Brian Statham, Trevor Bailey and overseas players not with our county teams, would give the league extra glamour and appeal.

Every showman seeks to produce this from his performers and cricket in the 1970's—certainly this sudden-death cricket—must woo the crowds.

I do not believe it is too late to settle the differences between the organisers of the Sunday League, the Counties and those responsible for running the Cavaliers. Perhaps in time for them to compete in the 1970 programme of matches?

Understandably there is uneasiness in some quarters that the advance of this instant-type cricket will hamper the development of the younger players.

I hope very much that, through sponsorship and Test matches, there will always be sufficient money available to continue the county championship. These one-day games, in themselves, are not enough to keep the best players in form.

Abroad it is comparatively easy for players to take part in a four-day match and then to come back after a break and play on yet another good wicket. In our conditions, regular play is essential if a young player is to learn his craft.

The Gillette Cup has helped to improve the game in one important aspect—the running between wickets. For the first 25 or 30 overs, the batsmen are inclined push for singles here and there. In fact, when you study the Gillette Cup and the way the runs are scored, you realise how many are missed or ignored every other day of the week in the county championship. This quick running, quite apart from its entertainment value and disruptive effect on fielding sides, develops a sense of urgency. I am all for encouraging young players to acquire this attitude rather than settle for accumulating runs by staid methods.

One-day cricket, with its guarantee of a result, usually brings in a fair-sized crowd, particularly on a Sunday and, of course, Test cricket, with odd exceptions, should always be a draw. Try getting a Test ticket for The Oval or Lord's!

Test cricket doesn't often provide the quick thrills of a one-day game, but no true cricket fan would want a Test match played in a slap-happy manner. Here are the best cricketers in the land playing against the elite of another nation. The pace of the game, to the untrained eye, must always seem slower, but the penalty for negligence, whether we like it or not, is usually banishment from the Test side, either for an aggravating period of months or even for ever.

While on the subject of Tests it is surely time for the 30 hours of play to be always available, if required, to complete a match.

Test matches could be scheduled to run from Wednesday to Monday, with Sunday and Tuesday as spare days, to be utilised if rain limited the hours of play in the intervening period.

I cannot see any problem in a Test commencing immediately after the end of a county match. After all, we play one game after another every week of the season. So, indeed, do the touring team.

Normally five days are ample. It is not often that you get so much rain that it would be necessary to take up the additional days.

Obviously there are some snags but, whatever they are, they must be considered comparatively minor when set against the importance of Test cricket. It does seem absurd that teams travel from one side of the world to the other expressly to compete in a Test series and then are denied the opportunity of definite results simply because the weather and rigid regulations do not make it possible to play the prescribed 30 hours.

# 20

# Sir 'Cricket'

LIFE moves so swiftly these days for a professional cricketer. There is barely time to relish what has just passed on tour before another major series is under way at home.

Often the contrast is striking between an England team playing abroad and an England team in action on its own soil.

You can field a successful side overseas and find that only four or five of that touring team are playing in the Tests the following summer. How can team spirit and confidence be sustained when players are discarded so quickly?

The Australians and the West Indies' selectors have the right idea. Once they place their faith in a player, he is kept in the Test squad. He may go three matches without achieving anything of note but all the time he is gathering Test experience. He is not under the mental pressure of knowing that, if he doesnt' succeed almost immediately, he is likely to be sacked from the team or the Test squad. The result, generally, is that he comes good.

In this country we do not always recognise the very narrow line between success and failure. We are too ready to drop a person if he doesn't come off in his first or second game.

I would like to see the following major changes made in our selection system:

The appointment of an overall team manager—A Sir Alf Ramsey of cricket if you like—who would be responsible for choosing all England teams, both at home and abroad.

The establishment of a squad of 18 to 20 players for each home Test series, who would come together at the end of March.

In suggesting a team manager to select teams, I am not advocating the disbandment of the existing four-man committee. They are all former players of vast experience and devote a tremendous amount of their time to travelling the country in search of possible Test material. They could still watch players but, instead of having the ultimate responsibility for naming the team, they would report back their recommendations to the manager. It would be his function to consider the various names put to him and to make the final selection.

I think the selectors in office during my career have done an excellent job, often in difficult circumstances. Nevertheless, I cannot believe it is an ideal arrangement to have four men managing the team which, in effect, is what has happened during home Test matches.

We have a system whereby the captain stands or falls by what he achieves on the field. Why not give similar terms of reference off the field to a team manager?

Players are more likely to identify themselves with one chief than four. If you had a personality such as Doug Insole or Mike Smith in sole charge of selection and management, you would surely have a better chance of breeding team spirit. He would, after all, not only be in control at home Tests but also on tour.

At the moment we have the curious situation of one set of people naming the England teams in this country, yet having no say in the selection of teams for matches played on tour. This is left to a tour manager, who is not normally a home selector. and a small committee consisting of the captain, the vice captain and possibly one other senior player.

Nor, indeed, do these home selectors see how the players perform overseas. They have to pick up the threads again when the team returns. Is it any wonder, therefore, that in a matter of a few months you can see so many changes taking place in the composition of an England Team?

I know it is argued in defence of this chopping and changing of team that players are picked according to their ability in certain conditions. There is some logic in this viewpoint. I would hope, however, that a sole manager would aim, in the long term, to develop players capable of playing in any conditions. If a Test player is at the top of his profession, he ought to be equipped to meet any situation.

This brings me to my second recommendation—the creation of a Test squad for home series.

It has always seemed a shame to me that the wonderful comradeship and spirit which touring teams enjoy should be allowed to evaporate once the tour is over.

In its place, you get the situation at home of newcomers coming into a Test team and only meeting their colleagues forty-eight hours or even less before the match. I remember Kenny Barrington telling me that, when he played in his first Test match some fourteen years ago, he felt very much the new boy. Few people in the team knew him and he wandered around feeling miserable.

I know the atmosphere has changed considerably in the past few years. Everybody helps everybody but, for the newcomers, it is still too brief a period to get to know the rest of the team.

That is why I would advocate a squad of say eighteen to twenty players being named towards the end of March. These players would form a Test party for the home series. They would have the whole of April and possible a week into May to train together.

Under the team manager they could digest the lessons of the most recent Test series. This would probably be the one in which many of them will have competed abroad that previous winter. They could analyse the strengths and weaknesses of their forthcoming opponents, using films and other data to assist them. They could also practise together at indoor school until the weather was suitable for net sessions at Lord's or one of the other Test grounds.

Ideally, the players in the squad not actually required for a particular Test, would remain with the team. I realise this would not appeal to some counties, especially those with several players in the Test squad. I think they would have to ask themselves: are our county commitments more important than the prestige of English cricket? They should not forget that they benefit considerably from Test match profits and the fees obtained from television and broadcasting.

When Colin Cowdrey returned from the West Indies in 1968 he paid a special tribute to the players who were not in the Test side. Much of the success of the tour, he maintained, was due to the wholehearted efforts and support given to the team by their off field colleagues.

We went a little way towards such a system against the Australians the next summer. Fifteen players were taken up for the first Test at Old Trafford. Critics complained this was too many, it confused the issue when it come to team selection and was the cause of England's defeat but I think the players appreciated the feeling of 'togetherness'. If I remember rightly, this was the word used by Sir Alf Ramsey when explaining one of the main reasons behind England's World Cup triumph at Wembley.

I know Colin Milburn was extremely grateful to be invited to the traditional eve of Test dinner before the third Test at Edgbaston. Colin had been injured during his fine innings at Lord's and was not available for Edgbaston. Not *available* but not *ignored*.

He was invited by the England selectors to join the England team in Birmingham for the match. He, and the rest of the squad, appreciated the gesture. I hope this is only the start.

With all round co-operation we could establish the same fine spirit of overseas tours for the home series. Sir Alf Ramsey proved it could work for England at Soccer. Give cricket's Overlord the same opportunity.

Meanwhile, if any lad loves this game enough to want a cricket career, there is opportunity enough for him. If we should meet, I hope that I can give him something of what cricket has given me.

# Appendix

## JOHN EDRICH

### Career Statistics compiled by Bill Frindall

ALL FIRST-CLASS MATCHES

BATTING & FIELDING

| *Season* | *M.* | *I.* | *N.O.* | *Runs* | *H.S.* | *Avge.* | *100s* | *50s* | *Catches* |
|---|---|---|---|---|---|---|---|---|---|
| 1956 | 3 | 6 | 0 | 34 | 14 | 5.66 | – | – | – |
| 1957 | 1 | 2 | 0 | 7 | 7 | 3.50 | – | – | – |
| 1958 | 1 | 1 | 1 | 24 | 24* | – | – | – | 1 |
| 1959 | 24 | 45 | 11 | 1799 | 126 | 52.91 | 7 | 5 | 8 |
| 1959–60 | 2 | 4 | 0 | 189 | 151 | 47.25 | 1 | – | – |
| 1960 | 30 | 52 | 3 | 1887 | 154 | 38.51 | 5 | 7 | 20 |
| 1961 | 31 | 58 | 0 | 1928 | 129 | 33.24 | 5 | 10 | 29 |
| 1962 | 30 | 55 | 7 | 2482 | 216 | 51.70 | 7 | 13 | 13 |
| 1962–3 | 5 | 10 | 0 | 425 | 136 | 42.50 | 1 | 2 | 3 |
| 1963 | 31 | 55 | 7 | 1921 | 125 | 40.02 | 2 | 12 | 19 |
| 1963–4 | 6 | 8 | 1 | 386 | 150 | 55.14 | 1 | – | 1 |
| 1964 | 26 | 45 | 3 | 1727 | 124 | 41.11 | 2 | 12 | 17 |
| 1965 | 28 | 44 | 7 | 2319 | 310* | 62.67 | 8 | 7 | 12 |
| 1965–6 | 16 | 25 | 1 | 1060 | 133 | 44.16 | 3 | 4 | 6 |
| 1966 | 28 | 49 | 3 | 1978 | 137 | 43.00 | 3 | 14 | 20 |
| 1967 | 31 | 47 | 5 | 2077 | 226* | 49.45 | 5 | 12 | 19 |
| 1967–8 | 10 | 17 | 1 | 739 | 146 | 46.18 | 1 | 5 | 5 |
| 1968 | 27 | 50 | 5 | 2009 | 164 | 44.64 | 5 | 10 | 18 |
| | 330 | 573 | 55 | 22991 | 310* | 44.38 | 56 | 113 | 191 |

(* *not out*)

BOWLING

| *Season* | *Overs* | *Maidens* | *Runs* | *Wickets* |
|---|---|---|---|---|
| 1961 | 0.1 | 0 | 4 | 0 |
| 1962–3 | 1 | 0 | 4 | 0 |
| 1963–4 | 5 | 1 | 27 | 0 |
| 1965 | 2 | 0 | 7 | 0 |
| 1965–6 | 1 | 0 | 6 | 0 |
| 1967 | 1 | 0 | 1 | 0 |
| | 10.1 | 1 | 49 | 0 |

OVERSEAS TOURS

1959–60 Surrey in Rhodesia.
1962–3 Cavaliers in South Africa and Rhodesia.
1963–4 MCC in India.
1965–6 MCC in Australia and New Zealand.
1967–8 MCC in West Indies.

HUNDREDS (56)

For ENGLAND (6)

| | |
|---|---|
| *v* Australia: | 120 at Lord's, 1964 (on début *v* Australia). |
| | 109 at Melbourne, 1965–6. |
| | 103 at Sydney, 1965–6. |
| | 164 at The Oval, 1968. |
| *v* New Zealand: | 310* at Leeds, 1965 (on début *v* New Zealand). |
| *v* West Indies: | 146 at Bridgetown, 1967–8. |

For SURREY (46)

John Edrich has scored a hundred against each of Surrey's sixteen County Championship opponents.

| | |
|---|---|
| *v* Derbyshire (1): | 125 at The Oval, 1963. |
| *v* Essex (3): | 103* at The Oval, 1959. |
| | 129 at Ilford, 1961. |
| | 161 at Chelmsford, 1967. |
| *v* Glamorgan (2): | 125 at The Oval, 1962. |
| | 100* at The Oval, 1967. |
| *v* Gloucestershire (1): | 205* at Bristol, 1965. |
| *v* Hampshire (2): | 105 at The Oval, 1961. |
| | 123 at The Oval, 1968. |
| *v* Kent (4): | 103 at The Oval, 1959. |
| | 113 at Blackheath, 1961. |
| | 113 at The Oval, 1962. |
| | 132 at Blackheath, 1966. |
| *v* Lancashire (1): | 136* at The Oval, 1966. |
| *v* Leicestershire (2): | 123 at Leicester, 1962. |
| | 129 at The Oval, 1968. |
| *v* Middlesex (4): | 125 at Lord's, 1960. |
| | 119 at Lord's, 1962. |
| | 226* at The Oval, 1967. |
| | 113 at Lord's, 1967. |
| *v* Northamptonshire (3): | 118 at The Oval, 1960. |
| | 107 at Northampton, 1961. |
| | 188 at Northampton, 1965. |

| | |
|---|---|
| *v* Nottinghamshire (5): | 112, 124 at Nottingham, 1959. |
| | 120 at Nottingham, 1960. |
| | 216 at Nottingham, 1962. |
| | 137 at Nottingham, 1966. |
| *v* Somerset (1): | 104* at The Oval, 1959. |
| *v* Sussex (1): | 180* at Hove, 1965. |
| *v* Warwickshire (1): | 154 at The Oval, 1960. |
| *v* Worcestershire (1): | 125 at Worcester, 1968. |
| *v* Yorkshire (4): | 103* at Sheffield, 1960. |
| | 154 at Sheffield, 1962. |
| | 124 at The Oval, 1964. |
| | 105 at Bradford, 1965. |
| *v* MCC (1): | 106 at Lord's, 1968. |
| *v* Cambridge University (3): | 126 at Guildford, 1959. |
| | 107 at The Oval, 1962. |
| | 101* at Cambridge, 1965. |
| *v* Oxford University (2): | 108 at The Oval, 1959. |
| | 121* at Oxford, 1965. |
| *v* Indians (1): | 108 at The Oval, 1967. |
| *v* New Zealanders (1): | 139 at The Oval, 1965. |
| *v* Rhodesia (1): | 151 at Bulawayo, 1959–60. |
| *v* West Indians (1): | 106* at The Oval, 1963. |

For MCC (2)

| | |
|---|---|
| *v* West Zone (1): | 150 at Ahmedabad, 1963–4. |
| *v* Queensland (1): | 133 at Brisbane, 1965–6. |

For T. N. PEARCE'S XI (1)

| | |
|---|---|
| *v* Australians (1): | 110 at Scarborough, 1961. |

For CAVALIERS (1)

| | |
|---|---|
| *v* Transvaal (1): | 136 at Johannesburg, 1962–3. |

AGGREGATES ON ENGLISH GROUNDS

| *Ground* | *M.* | *I.* | *N.O.* | *Runs* | *H.S.* | *Avge.* | *100s* | *50s* | *Catches* |
|---|---|---|---|---|---|---|---|---|---|
| Ashby-de-la-Zouch | 1 | 2 | 1 | 52 | 35* | 52.00 | – | – | – |
| Basingstoke | 1 | 2 | 0 | 14 | 8 | 7.00 | – | – | 1 |
| Bath | 2 | 4 | 1 | 131 | 84 | 43.66 | – | 1 | – |
| Birmingham | 5 | 10 | 0 | 356 | 94 | 35.60 | – | 3 | 3 |
| Blackheath | 6 | 12 | 1 | 555 | 132 | 50.45 | 2 | 2 | 1 |
| Bournemouth | 2 | 4 | 0 | 193 | 83 | 48.25 | – | 2 | 1 |
| Bradford | 4 | 6 | 0 | 263 | 105 | 43.83 | 1 | 1 | 2 |

AGGREGATES ON ENGLISH GROUNDS

| *Ground* | *M.* | *I.* | *N.O.* | *Runs* | *H.S.* | *Avge.* | *100s* | *50s* | *Catches* |
|---|---|---|---|---|---|---|---|---|---|
| Bristol | 1 | 1 | 1 | 205 | 205* | – | 1 | – | – |
| Buxton | 1 | 2 | 0 | 29 | 23 | 14.50 | – | – | 1 |
| Cambridge | 6 | 11 | 2 | 370 | 101* | 41.11 | 1 | 1 | 5 |
| Cardiff (Arms Park) | 4 | 7 | 0 | 227 | 78 | 32.42 | – | 2 | 3 |
| Chelmsford | 1 | 2 | 0 | 163 | 161 | 81.50 | 1 | – | – |
| Cheltenham | 1 | 2 | 0 | 35 | 33 | 17.50 | – | – | – |
| Chesterfield | 3 | 3 | 0 | 94 | 53 | 31.33 | – | 1 | 1 |
| Clacton | 1 | 1 | 0 | 73 | 73 | 73.00 | – | 1 | 1 |
| Coventry | 2 | 4 | 0 | 147 | 51 | 36.75 | – | 1 | 4 |
| Ebbw Vale | 1 | 2 | 0 | 47 | 36 | 23.50 | – | – | 3 |
| Gloucester | 3 | 6 | 1 | 133 | 45 | 26.60 | – | – | 2 |
| Gravesend | 1 | 1 | 0 | 17 | 17 | 17.00 | – | – | 1 |
| Guildford | 8 | 14 | 4 | 351 | 126 | 35.10 | 1 | 1 | 2 |
| Hove | 7 | 14 | 3 | 486 | 180* | 44.18 | 1 | 1 | 2 |
| Ilford | 2 | 4 | 0 | 186 | 129 | 46.50 | 1 | – | 1 |
| Leeds | 4 | 7 | 1 | 495 | 310* | 82.50 | 1 | 2 | 1 |
| Leicester | 6 | 10 | 0 | 455 | 123 | 45.50 | 1 | 3 | 4 |
| Leyton | 2 | 3 | 0 | 50 | 30 | 16.66 | – | – | – |
| Llanelly | 1 | 2 | 1 | 17 | 16* | 17.00 | – | – | – |
| Lord's | 33 | 56 | 5 | 2103 | 125 | 41.23 | 5 | 11 | 14 |
| Maidstone | 1 | 1 | 0 | 51 | 51 | 51.00 | – | 1 | 1 |
| Manchester | 7 | 13 | 0 | 269 | 49 | 20.69 | – | – | 5 |
| Northampton | 3 | 4 | 0 | 370 | 188 | 92.50 | 2 | 1 | 3 |
| Nottingham | 10 | 18 | 2 | 1203 | 216 | 75.18 | 5 | 5 | 11 |
| Nuneaton | 1 | – | – | – | – | – | – | – | – |
| Oval | 125 | 216 | 24 | 8380 | 226* | 43.64 | 21 | 45 | 79 |
| Oxford | 2 | 2 | 1 | 201 | 121* | 201.00 | 1 | 1 | 1 |
| Portsmouth | 1 | 2 | 0 | 13 | 13 | 6.50 | – | – | – |
| Romford | 2 | 4 | 1 | 151 | 49* | 50.33 | – | – | 2 |
| Scarborough | 11 | 21 | 1 | 856 | 110 | 42.80 | 1 | 7 | 6 |
| Sheffield | 3 | 6 | 1 | 319 | 154 | 63.80 | 2 | – | – |
| Southampton | 3 | 5 | 0 | 162 | 84 | 32.40 | – | 2 | 2 |
| Southend | 1 | 2 | 0 | 96 | 61 | 48.00 | – | 1 | 1 |
| Southport | 1 | 2 | 0 | 12 | 10 | 6.00 | – | – | 2 |
| Swansea | 1 | 2 | 0 | 17 | 9 | 8.50 | – | – | – |
| Taunton | 1 | 2 | 0 | 184 | 95 | 92.00 | – | 2 | 1 |
| Weston-Super-Mare | 2 | 4 | 1 | 139 | 60* | 46.33 | – | 1 | 2 |
| Worcester | 7 | 13 | 0 | 522 | 125 | 40.15 | 1 | 3 | 7 |
| Totals | 291 | 509 | 52 | 20192 | 310* | 44.18 | 49 | 102 | 176 |

## AGGREGATES ON OVERSEAS GROUNDS

### (i) In AUSTRALIA

| *Ground* | *M.* | *I.* | *N.O.* | *Runs* | *H.S.* | *Avge.* | *100s* | *50s* | *Catches* |
|---|---|---|---|---|---|---|---|---|---|
| Adelaide | 2 | 4 | 0 | 96 | 61 | 24.00 | – | 1 | 2 |
| Brisbane | 2 | 4 | 1 | 270 | 133 | 90.00 | 1 | 1 | – |
| Hobart | 1 | 1 | 0 | 1 | 1 | 1.00 | – | – | – |
| Melbourne | 3 | 5 | 0 | 244 | 109 | 48.80 | 1 | 1 | 3 |
| Perth | 2 | 4 | 0 | 180 | 92 | 45.00 | – | 1 | – |
| Sydney | 2 | 3 | 0 | 186 | 103 | 62.00 | 1 | – | – |
| Totals | 12 | 21 | 1 | 977 | 133 | 48.85 | 3 | 4 | 5 |

### (ii) In INDIA

| *Ground* | *M.* | *I.* | *N.O.* | *Runs* | *H.S.* | *Avge.* | *100s* | *50s* | *Catches* |
|---|---|---|---|---|---|---|---|---|---|
| Ahmedabad | 1 | 1 | 0 | 150 | 150 | 150.00 | 1 | – | – |
| Amritsar | 1 | 2 | 1 | 49 | 39* | 49.00 | – | – | – |
| Hyderabad | 1 | 1 | 0 | 32 | 32 | 32.00 | – | – | – |
| Kanpur | 1 | 1 | 0 | 35 | 35 | 35.00 | – | – | 1 |
| Nagpur | 1 | 2 | 0 | 79 | 42 | 39.50 | – | – | – |
| New Delhi | 1 | 1 | 0 | 41 | 41 | 41.00 | – | – | – |
| Totals | 6 | 8 | 1 | 386 | 150 | 55.14 | 1 | – | 1 |

### (iii) In NEW ZEALAND

| *Ground* | *M.* | *I.* | *N.O.* | *Runs* | *H.S.* | *Avge.* | *100s* | *50s* | *Catches* |
|---|---|---|---|---|---|---|---|---|---|
| Auckland | 1 | – | – | – | – | – | – | – | – |
| Christchurch | 1 | 2 | 0 | 4 | 2 | 2.00 | – | – | – |
| Dunedin | 1 | 1 | 0 | 36 | 36 | 36.00 | – | – | – |
| Wellington | 1 | 1 | 0 | 43 | 43 | 43.00 | – | – | 1 |
| Totals | 4 | 4 | 0 | 83 | 43 | 20.75 | – | – | 1 |

### (iv) In SOUTH AFRICA & RHODESIA

| *Ground* | *M.* | *I.* | *N.O.* | *Runs* | *H.S.* | *Avge.* | *100s* | *50s* | *Catches* |
|---|---|---|---|---|---|---|---|---|---|
| Bulawayo | 1 | 2 | 0 | 166 | 151 | 83.00 | 1 | – | – |
| Cape Town | 1 | 2 | 0 | 13 | 12 | 6.50 | – | – | – |
| Johannesburg | 2 | 4 | 0 | 299 | 136 | 77.25 | 1 | 2 | 1 |
| Port Elizabeth | 1 | 2 | 0 | 61 | 34 | 30.50 | – | – | 2 |
| Salisbury | 2 | 4 | 0 | 75 | 47 | 18.75 | – | – | – |
| Totals | 7 | 14 | 0 | 614 | 151 | 43.85 | 2 | 2 | 3 |

(v) In The WEST INDIES

| *Ground* | *M.* | *I.* | *N.O.* | *Runs* | *H.S.* | *Avge.* | *100s* | *50s* | *Catches* |
|---|---|---|---|---|---|---|---|---|---|
| Bridgetown | 3 | 4 | 0 | 244 | 146 | 61.00 | 1 | 1 | – |
| Georgetown | 2 | 4 | 1 | 91 | 60* | 30.33 | – | 1 | 2 |
| Kingston | 2 | 4 | 0 | 224 | 98 | 56.00 | – | 2 | 2 |
| Port of Spain | 3 | 5 | 0 | 180 | 67 | 36.00 | – | 1 | 1 |
| Totals | 10 | 17 | 1 | 739 | 146 | 46.18 | 1 | 5 | 5 |

COMPLETE CAREER AGGREGATES

| | *M.* | *I.* | *N.O.* | *Runs* | *H.S.* | *Avge.* | *100s* | *50s* | *Catches* |
|---|---|---|---|---|---|---|---|---|---|
| In Australia | 12 | 21 | 1 | 977 | 133 | 48.85 | 3 | 4 | 5 |
| In India | 6 | 8 | 1 | 386 | 150 | 55.14 | 1 | – | 1 |
| In New Zealand | 4 | 4 | 0 | 83 | 43 | 20.75 | – | – | 1 |
| In Southern Africa | 7 | 14 | 0 | 614 | 151 | 43.85 | 2 | 2 | 3 |
| In West Indies | 10 | 17 | 1 | 739 | 146 | 46.18 | 1 | 5 | 5 |
| Overseas Totals | 39 | 64 | 3 | 2799 | 151 | 45.88 | 7 | 11 | 15 |
| In England | 291 | 509 | 52 | 20192 | 310* | 44.18 | 49 | 102 | 176 |
| Career Totals | 330 | 573 | 55 | 22991 | 310* | 44.38 | 56 | 113 | 191 |

METHOD OF DISMISSAL

| | |
|---|---|
| Bowled | 85 |
| Caught | 345 |
| LBW | 62 |
| Stumped | 13 |
| Run Out | 12 |
| Hit Wicket | 1 |
| Totals | 518 |

HUNDRED PARTNERSHIPS

| | | *Wicket* | | | | | | | | | |
|---|---|---|---|---|---|---|---|---|---|---|---|
| *For* | *Total* | *1st* | *2nd* | *3rd* | *4th* | *5th* | *6th* | *7th* | *8th* | *9th* | *10th* |
| England | 11 | 2 | 3 | 2 | 3 | 1 | – | – | – | – | – |
| Surrey | 69 | 33 | 19 | 13 | 3 | – | 1 | – | – | – | – |
| MCC | 11 | 5 | 4 | 2 | – | – | – | – | – | – | – |
| Players | 2 | – | 2 | – | – | – | – | – | – | – | – |
| Cavaliers | 1 | – | – | – | 1 | – | – | – | – | – | – |
| T. N. Pearce's XI | 1 | 1 | – | – | – | – | – | – | – | – | – |
| Totals | 95 | 41 | 28 | 17 | 7 | 1 | 1 | – | – | – | – |

In all first-class matches, Edrich has shared 21 century partnerships with M. J. Stewart, 20 with K. F. Barrington, and 11 with M. J. Edwards.

HUNDRED BEFORE LUNCH (1)

110 for T. N. Pearce's XI *v* Australians (Scarborough) 1961. (On the first day)

HUNDRED IN BOTH INNINGS OF A MATCH (1)
112 & 124 Surrey *v* Nottinghamshire (Nottingham) 1959
(His second County Championship match)

CARRYING BAT THROUGH A COMPLETED INNINGS (1)
79* out of 122 for Surrey *v* Northamptonshire (Oval) 1963

DUCKS

| | |
|---|---|
| For England | 3 |
| For Surrey | 21 |
| For other teams | 3 |
| Total | 27 |

Edrich has twice been dismissed for a 'pair' and each instance occurred at The Oval, the first being his début on the ground:
1956 for Combined Services *v* Surrey
1961 for Surrey *v* Australians

## TEST MATCHES

### (Début: 1963 *v* West Indies at Old Trafford, Manchester)

BATTING & FIELDING

| *Season* | *Against* | *M.* | *I.* | *N.O.* | *Runs* | *H.S.* | *Avge.* | *100s* | *50s* | *Catches* |
|---|---|---|---|---|---|---|---|---|---|---|
| 1963 | West Indies | 3 | 6 | 0 | 103 | 38 | 17.16 | – | – | 2 |
| 1963–4 | India | 2 | 2 | 0 | 76 | 41 | 38.00 | – | – | 1 |
| 1964 | Australia | 3 | 4 | 0 | 161 | 120 | 40.25 | 1 | – | 1 |
| 1965 | New Zealand | 1 | 1 | 1 | 310 | 310* | – | 1 | – | – |
| 1965 | South Africa | 1 | 2 | 1 | 7 | 7* | 7.00 | – | – | 1 |
| 1965–6 | Australia | 5 | 8 | 0 | 375 | 109 | 46.88 | 2 | 1 | 4 |
| 1965–6 | New Zealand | 3 | 3 | 0 | 40 | 36 | 13.33 | – | – | – |
| 1966 | West Indies | 1 | 1 | 0 | 35 | 35 | 35.00 | – | – | 1 |
| 1967 | India | 2 | 3 | 0 | 35 | 22 | 11.66 | – | – | 1 |
| 1967–8 | West Indies | 5 | 8 | 0 | 340 | 146 | 42.50 | 1 | 1 | 4 |
| 1968 | Australia | 5 | 9 | 0 | 554 | 164 | 61.55 | 1 | 4 | 2 |
| Totals | | 31 | 47 | 2 | 2036 | 310* | 45.24 | 6 | 6 | 17 |

| *Against* | *M.* | *I.* | *N.O.* | *Runs* | *H.S.* | *Avge.* | *100s* | *50s* | *Catches* |
|---|---|---|---|---|---|---|---|---|---|
| Australia | 13 | 21 | 0 | 1090 | 164 | 51.90 | 4 | 5 | 7 |
| South Africa | 1 | 2 | 1 | 7 | 7* | 7.00 | – | – | 1 |
| West Indies | 9 | 15 | 0 | 478 | 146 | 31.86 | 1 | 1 | 7 |
| New Zealand | 4 | 4 | 1 | 350 | 310* | 116.66 | 1 | – | – |
| India | 4 | 5 | 0 | 111 | 41 | 22.20 | – | – | 2 |
| Totals | 31 | 47 | 2 | 2036 | 310* | 45.24 | 6 | 6 | 17 |

| | M. | I. | N.O. | Runs | H.S. | Avge. | 100s | 50s | Catches |
|---|---|---|---|---|---|---|---|---|---|
| In England | 16 | 26 | 2 | 1205 | 310* | 50.20 | 3 | 4 | 8 |
| Overseas | 15 | 21 | 0 | 831 | 146 | 39.57 | 3 | 2 | 9 |
| Totals | 31 | 47 | 2 | 2036 | 310* | 45.24 | 6 | 6 | 17 |

BOWLING

| Season | Against | Overs | Maidens | Runs | Wickets |
|---|---|---|---|---|---|
| 1963–4 | India | 4 | 1 | 17 | 0 |
| 1965–6 | New Zealand | 1 | 0 | 6 | 0 |
| Totals | | 5 | 1 | 23 | 0 |

HUNDRED PARTNERSHIPS (11)

| Season | Against | Total | Wicket | Partner | Venue |
|---|---|---|---|---|---|
| 1965 | New Zealand | 369 | 2nd | K. F. Barrington | Leeds |
| 1965–6 | Australia | 118 | 3rd | K. F. Barrington | Melbourne |
| | | 105 | 4th | M. C. Cowdrey | Melbourne |
| | | 178 | 3rd | K. F. Barrington | Melbourne |
| 1967–8 | West Indies | 129 | 2nd | M. C. Cowdrey | Kingston |
| | | 172 | 1st | G. Boycott | Bridgetown |
| | | 109 | 4th | T. W. Graveney | Bridgetown |
| 1968 | Australia | 108 | 2nd | M. C. Cowdrey | Birmingham |
| | | 123 | 1st | R. M. Prideaux | Leeds |
| | | 125 | 4th | T. W. Graveney | Oval |
| | | 121 | 5th | B. L. D'Oliveira | Oval |

## COUNTY CHAMPIONSHIP MATCHES

| Season | M. | I. | N.O. | Runs | H.S. | Avge. | 100s | 50s | Ct. | Runs | Wkts. |
|---|---|---|---|---|---|---|---|---|---|---|---|
| 1958 | 1 | 1 | 1 | 24 | 24* | – | – | – | 1 | – | – |
| 1959 | 21 | 39 | 9 | 1432 | 124 | 47.73 | 5 | 4 | 8 | – | – |
| 1960 | 21 | 34 | 3 | 1424 | 154 | 45.93 | 5 | 5 | 14 | – | – |
| 1961 | 22 | 42 | 0 | 1502 | 129 | 35.76 | 4 | 8 | 19 | 4 | 0 |
| 1962 | 21 | 38 | 4 | 1674 | 216 | 49.23 | 6 | 6 | 8 | – | – |
| 1963 | 22 | 39 | 6 | 1330 | 125 | 40.30 | 1 | 9 | 15 | – | – |
| 1964 | 20 | 35 | 3 | 1328 | 124 | 41.50 | 1 | 10 | 16 | – | – |
| 1965 | 21 | 34 | 2 | 1513 | 205* | 47.28 | 4 | 6 | 10 | 7 | 0 |
| 1966 | 24 | 44 | 3 | 1913 | 137 | 46.65 | 3 | 14 | 17 | – | – |
| 1967 | 24 | 36 | 5 | 1658 | 226* | 53.48 | 4 | 9 | 14 | 1 | 0 |
| 1968 | 18 | 34 | 3 | 1114 | 129 | 35.93 | 3 | 4 | 15 | – | – |
| | 215 | 376 | 39 | 14912 | 226* | 44.24 | 36 | 75 | 137 | 12 | 0 |

| *Against* | *M.* | *I.* | *N.O.* | *Runs* | *H.S.* | *Avge.* | *100s* | *50s* | *Ct.* | *Runs* | *Wkts.* |
|---|---|---|---|---|---|---|---|---|---|---|---|
| Derbyshire | 12 | 19 | 3 | 657 | 125 | 41.06 | 1 | 3 | 9 | – | – |
| Essex | 16 | 28 | 3 | 1215 | 161 | 48.60 | 3 | 4 | 7 | 7 | 0 |
| Glamorgan | 12 | 20 | 3 | 642 | 125 | 37.76 | 2 | 2 | 10 | – | – |
| Gloucestershire | 10 | 17 | 2 | 584 | 205* | 38.93 | 1 | 1 | 7 | – | – |
| Hampshire | 12 | 23 | 0 | 846 | 123 | 36.78 | 2 | 6 | 7 | – | – |
| Kent | 16 | 29 | 2 | 1316 | 132 | 48.74 | 4 | 8 | 11 | – | – |
| Lancashire | 10 | 19 | 4 | 395 | 136* | 26.33 | 1 | 1 | 6 | 1 | 0 |
| Leicestershire | 12 | 20 | 2 | 829 | 129 | 46.05 | 2 | 5 | 7 | – | – |
| Middlesex | 16 | 30 | 2 | 1500 | 226* | 53.57 | 4 | 9 | 8 | – | – |
| Northamptonshire | 10 | 16 | 2 | 895 | 188 | 63.92 | 3 | 4 | 8 | – | – |
| Nottinghamshire | 18 | 30 | 3 | 1580 | 216 | 58.51 | 5 | 9 | 18 | – | – |
| Somerset | 11 | 22 | 4 | 973 | 104* | 54.05 | 1 | 8 | 6 | – | – |
| Sussex | 15 | 28 | 5 | 770 | 180* | 33.47 | 1 | 3 | 4 | 4 | 0 |
| Warwickshire | 13 | 21 | 0 | 754 | 154 | 35.90 | 1 | 3 | 8 | – | – |
| Worcestershire | 16 | 27 | 2 | 981 | 125 | 39.24 | 1 | 6 | 13 | – | – |
| Yorkshire | 16 | 27 | 2 | 975 | 154 | 39.00 | 4 | 3 | 8 | – | – |
| | 215 | 376 | 39 | 14912 | 226* | 44.24 | 36 | 75 | 137 | 12 | 0 |

| | *M.* | *I.* | *N.O.* | *Runs* | *H.S.* | *Avge.* | *100s* | *50s* | *Ct.* | *Runs* | *Wkts.* |
|---|---|---|---|---|---|---|---|---|---|---|---|
| Home Matches | 110 | 188 | 24 | 6930 | 226* | 42.25 | 15 | 37 | 68 | 11 | 0 |
| Away Matches | 105 | 188 | 15 | 7982 | 216 | 46.13 | 21 | 38 | 69 | 1 | 0 |
| | 215 | 376 | 39 | 14912 | 226* | 44.24 | 36 | 75 | 137 | 12 | 0 |

## ALL MATCHES FOR SURREY

| | M. | I. | N.O. | Runs | H.S. | Avge. | 100s | 50s | Ct. | Runs | Wkts. |
|---|---|---|---|---|---|---|---|---|---|---|---|
| Championship | 215 | 376 | 39 | 14912 | 226* | 44.24 | 36 | 75 | 136 | 12 | 0 |
| v MCC | 9 | 12 | 0 | 416 | 106 | 34.66 | 1 | 1 | 4 | – | – |
| v Cambridge U. | 9 | 16 | 4 | 725 | 126 | 60.41 | 3 | 2 | 7 | – | – |
| v Oxford U. | 6 | 9 | 1 | 601 | 121* | 75.12 | 2 | 5 | 3 | – | – |
| v Australians | 4 | 8 | 1 | 220 | 76* | 31.42 | – | 2 | 2 | – | – |
| v Indians | 1 | 2 | 0 | 113 | 108 | 56.50 | 1 | – | 2 | – | – |
| v New Zealand | 1 | 2 | 0 | 139 | 139 | 69.50 | 1 | – | – | – | – |
| v Pakistanis | 1 | 2 | 0 | 67 | 57 | 33.50 | – | 1 | – | – | – |
| v Rhodesia | 2 | 4 | 0 | 189 | 151 | 47.25 | 1 | – | – | – | – |
| v South Africans | 1 | 2 | 0 | 12 | 12 | 6.00 | – | – | 1 | – | – |
| v West Indians | 2 | 3 | 1 | 185 | 106* | 92.50 | 1 | 1 | 2 | – | – |
| | 251 | 436 | 46 | 17579 | 226* | 45.07 | 46 | 87 | 157 | 12 | 0 |